全国高等职业院校外语类"十三五"规划教材

交际英语 视听说

English Communication
Through Watching, Listening & Speaking

主 编 王 颖
副主编 郭晓丽

http://www.hustp.com
中国·武汉

内 容 简 介

本教材包括10个单元,每个单元围绕着一个主题让学生完成相关的交际任务。教材中的主题来自于对学生、企业人士和教师的问卷调查。教材基于MUFC教学理念——M(meaning)、U(use)、F(form)和C(communication),为学生量身设计各种任务。每个单元的主要内容包括:①主题导入。导入的方式可能是相关口语活动、主题讨论、听音频或看视频,目的是为了帮助学生熟悉与主题相关的知识和语言,激发学习兴趣,为接下来的课堂听说活动热身。②音频、视频学习。包括背景介绍、场景介绍,为学生充分理解材料中的语言和内容做好准备。③交际任务。本教材根据交际目的来设计学习任务。学生通过协商来完成任务,通过表达他们的态度和情感来解决问题。④词汇习得。学生完成每个单元的词汇练习。每个单元建立的口语高频词词库可以有效地帮助学生积累词汇。

本教材适合作为大专院校低年级学生的英语视听说教材,同时也为广大英语爱好者、自学者提供了一种提高英语听说能力、培养职业软技能的选择。

图书在版编目(CIP)数据

交际英语视听说/王颖主编.—武汉:华中科技大学出版社,2018.1(2023.9重印)
ISBN 978-7-5680-3605-4

Ⅰ.①交… Ⅱ.①王… Ⅲ.①英语-口语 Ⅳ.①H319.9

中国版本图书馆 CIP 数据核字(2018)第 002406 号

交际英语视听说　　　　　　　　　　　　　　　　　　王　颖　主编
Jiaoji Yingyu Shitingshuo

策划编辑:李　欢
责任编辑:刘　平
封面设计:刘　婷
责任校对:张会军
责任监印:周治超

出版发行:华中科技大学出版社(中国·武汉)　　电话:(027)81321913
　　　　　武汉市东湖新技术开发区华工科技园　　邮编:430223
录　　排:华中科技大学惠友文印中心
印　　刷:武汉市籍缘印刷厂
开　　本:787mm×1092mm　1/16
印　　张:8.25　插页:1
字　　数:145千字
版　　次:2023年9月第1版第4次印刷
定　　价:36.00元

本书若有印装质量问题,请向出版社营销中心调换
全国免费服务热线:400-6679-118　　竭诚为您服务
版权所有　侵权必究

前　言

《大学英语课程教学要求》提到，"大学英语的教学目标是培养学生的英语综合应用能力，特别是听说能力，使他们在今后学习、工作和社会交往中能用英语有效地进行交际，同时增强其自主学习能力，提高综合文化素养，以适应我国社会发展和国际交流的需要。"因此，本教材旨在通过有效的视听手段提高学生的英语交际能力。本教材有如下特点：

1. 真实素材保证教材的真实性、地道性和趣味性

教材组收集了多部影视脚本，建立了影视脚本语料库，并从中选取了具有教学意义的高频词汇，截取相对应的视频，再结合学生特点设计相应的教学任务，帮助学生有效提高口语能力。

2. 主题选取贴近学生生活，确保学生的参与度

本教材的每个单元都有一个主题，这些主题都是通过采访在校生、往届的毕业生、企业人士和授课教师总结提炼出来的，贴近学生生活。学生在完成每个主题的任务时，都会感觉有话可说，有事可做，并且这些主题的训练对学生毕业后的工作和生活有所帮助。

3. 功能教学保证教材的实用性

本教材不是单纯练习口语词汇，而是通过每个单元的活动让学生操练语言。本教材以学生交际目的为依据选择语言项目，并根据交际目的来确定学生应该学习的交际功能。选择的功能都是绝大多数交际场合都需要的，如问候、提建议、做决定等。

4. 任务设计符合学生认知规律

本教材设计的任务接近人们在日常生活或工作中使用语言的真实情况，学生在完成任务后会得到一个最终产品(final product)。学生通过协商来完成任务，注意力都集中在如何解决问题上而不是使用哪些语言形式。在执行任务的过程中学生可以表达他们的态度和情感。

5. 技能培养提高学生的职业核心能力

一个学生的全面发展光有语言知识是不够的，软技能能够帮助学生学会如何处理人际关系，如何有效沟通。这些技能可以帮助学生在未来的职场道路上扫清障碍。编者在每一个单元中都精心设计了各种任务来培养学生的软技能。

本教材由深圳信息职业技术学院王颖主编，深圳信息职业技术学院郭晓丽担任副主编。王颖负责大纲的拟定和统稿定稿，并编写了第一单元到第五单元；郭晓丽与王颖共同编写了第六单元到第十单元。

本教材在编写过程中，得到了外教 Haidee 的大力支持，以及华中科技大学出版社的专业指导，编者在此深表谢意！

受时间和编者水平的限制，本书难免有不足之处，敬请专家和读者指正。

编者
2017 年 10 月

For Students

Dear Students,

If you want to speak English fluently, maybe the following tips can help you.

1. Understand that there is no **"magic bullet"**.

That means there is NO secret and super-effective way to guarantee fluency very fast.

If anyone says they have "the secret" to instant fluency... don't believe them!

2. Use English in your **daily life** as much as possible.

Using English for 10 minutes a day, every day, is better than studying for 1 hour only once a week. Here are a few suggestions for making English part of your daily life:

  • Listen to English as you walk to school.

  • Read the news online in English instead of in your native language.

  • Read articles, listen to podcasts, and watch videos in English about the topics you enjoy.

3. Learn to **think in English.**

This is one of the best ways to practice English, because if you make a "mistake", nobody knows about it! Also, you can practice thinking in English anytime, anywhere. No need for a textbook or classroom. The earlier you begin the habit of thinking in English, the easier it will be to speak fast.

4. Don't think too much about grammar, and don't worry about mistakes.

One of the biggest "mental blocks" for English learners is being nervous or afraid to **make a mistake** or embarrassed if they don't speak perfectly. But remember: Communication is MUCH more important than perfection!

5. Don't give up... never stop learning!

I've had a lot of students who study for a few years, then stop... then start again, then stop for a long time, then re-start... maybe you have done this, too. The problem is that you often lose the progress you made before, and then becoming fluent takes much, much longer.

6. Focus on **high frequency phrases.**

  • What are high frequency phrases?

They are combinations of words which are used together with greater than usual frequency. Here are some examples:

latest gossip	adjective＋noun
package tour	noun＋noun
have a great time	verb＋adjective＋noun
discuss calmly	verb＋adverb
completely satisfied	adverb＋adjective
figure out	phrasal verbs / idioms

Actions speak louder than words.

- Why should phrases be taught and learnt?

1) Words don't come singly.

2) High frequency phrases can make communication quicker, easier and more relaxed.

- How to study high frequency phrases?

The most effective strategy is to learn them **one at a time**. Ask yourself the following questions.

- Do you keep a high frequency phrase notebook?
- What's the best way to record high frequency phrases so you can remember them?
- How often do you review the meaning of the high frequency phrases you have learned?
- Do you create your own example sentences?

High frequency phrases are less formal, easier to understand and everyone uses them! Spoken English is stuffed with them and if you're serious about **improving your spoken English** you definitely need to pay attention to them.

Contents

Unit 1 Getting Started 1
   Part 1 What do you know about college life? 1
   Part 2 Getting to know yourself 2
   Part 3 Lyrics for your reference 7
   Part 4 My own dictionary 10

Unit 2 Silver Linings 14
   Part 1 Life problems 14
   Part 2 How to make a suggestion 15
   Part 3 Dear Abby 17
   Part 4 Hand tracing 20
   Part 5 Lyrics for your reference 20
   Part 6 My own dictionary 24

Unit 3 Living in the Moment 27
   Part 1 Happiness survey 27
   Part 2 Ways to be happier 28
   Part 3 Scripts for your reference 38
   Part 4 My own dictionary 40

Unit 4 Wanderlust 44
   Part 1 Dream destinations 44
   Part 2 Agreeing and disagreeing 46
   Part 3 Let's go! 47
   Part 4 My own dictionary 49

Unit 5 Shopping Season — 53

Part 1	Luxury or bargain?	53
Part 2	How do you spend your money?	54
Part 3	Gift certificate or coupon	57
Part 4	My own dictionary	60

Unit 6 A New Me — 63

Part 1	New Year's resolution	63
Part 2	Keep your New Year's resolution	65
Part 3	Your New Year's resolution	67
Part 4	Scripts for your reference	69
Part 5	My own dictionary	71

Unit 7 Life Is a Hobby — 76

Part 1	What do you have in common?	76
Part 2	Taking up a new hobby	78
Part 3	Talking about hobbies	82
Part 4	Dialogues about hobbies	83
Part 5	My own dictionary	86

Unit 8 Culture Awareness — 90

Part 1	What is culture?	90
Part 2	Importance of cultural awareness	93
Part 3	Right attitude	95
Part 4	My own dictionary	97

Unit 9 Creative Selling — 101

Part 1	How to sell a product	101
Part 2	Make it possible	102
Part 3	How to think outside of the box	104
Part 4	Red Dot Award	105
Part 5	Ways for your reference to be more creative	106
Part 6	My own dictionary	108

Contents

Unit 10 Job Interview   110

    Part 1   Different jobs ··· 110

    Part 2   Job interview ··· 112

    Part 3   Scripts for your reference ··· 115

    Part 4   My own dictionary ·· 119

Unit 1　Getting Started

Part 1　What do you know about college life?

1.1　Work in pairs

Work with your partner and write down anything occurring to you about college.

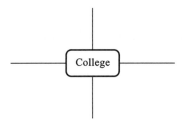

1.2　Read

Read about the differences between life in high school and life in college.

	High School	College
Class Time and Free Time	• You need to spend 30 or more hours a week in the classroom. • The teachers keep control of the students' time.	• You take a load of 15-20 hours of class a week. • You must manage your own time and **make** your own **decisions**.
Responsibility	• Your parents take good care of you by preparing your meals and making sure that you are healthy.	• You must **take responsibility for** your own life. You do your laundry, **get along with** your roommates.

续表

	High School	College
Teacher vs. Professor	• The teachers **get in touch with** the students who are struggling or missing work. • If you are absent, the teachers let you know what you have missed.	• If the students have problems, they can **make an appointment with** their teachers to **work it out**. • If you are absent, the college professors expect you to get the information from your classmates.
Testing and Grading	• The students **go through** a lot of tests.	• There are only one or two tests in one term, so the students should avoid missing the exam.

Part 2　Getting to know yourself

2.1　Write

College is a wonderful time for young people, but **it won't be easy**. You will experience some **ups and downs**, frustrations and anxieties, so it's **critically important** to find yourself.

Choose one aspect of your present situation you are unhappy with.

- It's difficult for me to _____
- I'm going to try to _____
- I can't _____

Now, try using other expressions to sound more positive.

- It's a challenge for me to _____
- I'm going to _____
- I'm sure that _____

2.2　Prepare for group work

How self-confident are you?

1. How do you react when you're meeting someone **for the first time** who you are trying to impress?

   a. **at a loss for words** and palms of your hands start to sweat

   b. overanxious to please

   c. witty and **in command of the situation**

2. Who do you feel most relaxed with?

   a. with a crowd

   b. with one or two close friends

   c. **on your own** with a good book to read

3. What would you do if you were having trouble in finding a street address?

   a. ask somebody of your own age and sex

   b. do your best to **work it out** from the map

   c. ask the first intelligent-looking person you see

4. How do you react at job interviews?

   a. **look the interviewer straight in the eye** and speak clearly

   b. speak very quietly and **keep looking at** the floor

   c. hide your nerves by talking loudly

5. Which way would you **prefer to** express your love for someone?

   a. in person

   b. on the phone

   c. in a letter

6. How do you **react to** compliments?

   a. blush and feel self-conscious

   b. question their sincerity and doubting what they say

   c. **find a way** to compliment them **in return**

7. What would you do if a television crew was doing a street interview?

   a. give an interview and **kick yourself** afterwards for not having said everything you want to

   b. express your opinions confidently and clearly

   c. avoid being asked by crossing the road

8. How do you react to someone you meet in a lift?

   a. avoid all eye-contact

   b. talk about the weather

   c. **crack a joke**

9. How do you react if somebody uses offensive language?

   a. tell them to **clean up** their language

   b. it upsets you and you leave

   c. pretend not to notice

10. Who would you **turn to** if you had a crisis in your personal life?

    a. nobody

    b. a close friend or relative

    c. **phone up** a counseling service

Keys and points

1. a-3 b-2 c-1   4. a-1 b-3 c-2   7. a-2 b-1 c-3   10. a-3 b-1 c-2

2. a-1 b-2 c-3   5. a-1 b-3 c-2   8. a-3 b-2 c-1

3. a-2 b-3 c-1   6. a-3 b-2 c-1   9. a-1 b-2 c-3

What your score means

0-10   You **tend to** be over-confident **at times**. Generally speaking, you **get on** very well with people **as long as** you remain sensitive to their needs.

11-20   Yours is the typical human condition. Sometimes you can be quite pushy and outgoing, and other times rather reticent. And even you're occasionally a little self-conscious, it's probably a lot more attractive to other people than you realize.

21-30   You seem to worry too much about what other people think of you. **In reality**, they are just probably just as shy as you are and there's no justification for your concern. **Instead of** concentrating on the impression you're making, try to **get outside of yourself** by thinking more about other people you meet, and what their problem might be.

Share your score with your partner or group member.

2.3 Small talk

Watch the video and study the short conversations.

1. Alright Matt! How's it going?

   Yeah, no trouble. How about you—alright?

   Yeah, not bad! I haven't seen you **for ages**!

   No, no—I've been busy, aren't I?

2. Hey Jane, how're you doing?

   Good thanks, and you?

   Yeah, not bad, not bad. **What are you up to**?

   Oh, this and that...just the usual! What about you?

3. Alright Carrie, how are you?

   Yeah, I'm fine. Neil, how are you going?

   Yeah, very well. **What are you doing around here**?

   Oh, I was just popping into the shop down the road there.

Saying hello	How do you do?
	Pleased to meet you. / Nice to meet you.
	Long time no see.
	Nice to see you.
	All right?
	How are you doing? / How's it going?
Saying goodbye	Take care. / Mind how you go.
	It's a pleasure talking to you. / It was great speaking to you.
	Safe journey.
	So long. / See you around. /(I'll) be seeing you.
	See you. / See you later. / Catch you later.

Practice these small talk expressions in a game of Round Robin. You can share your score with your partner. Try to be as confident as you can be.

2.4 Work in pairs

What is your character?

Character description	Always	Often	Sometimes	Rarely	Never
1. You **get along with** others, but sometimes you have a **selfish streak**.	☐	☐	☐	☐	☐
2. You have **an outgoing personality** and **a good sense of humor**.	☐	☐	☐	☐	☐
3. You have **a vivid imagination**, but you tend to **lose your temper** too easily.	☐	☐	☐	☐	☐
4. You are **highly intelligent** with **a razor-sharp mind**. You make things work.	☐	☐	☐	☐	☐
5. You **set high standards** for yourself and you **take** friendship **seriously**.	☐	☐	☐	☐	☐
6. The best aspect of your personality is the way you always **put others first**.	☐	☐	☐	☐	☐
7. Although you can be **painfully shy** in social situations, at work you **give the impression** of being **supremely confident**.	☐	☐	☐	☐	☐
8. You **tend** to make **snap decisions**.	☐	☐	☐	☐	☐
9. You have a strong **sense of responsibility** and always **keep your word**.	☐	☐	☐	☐	☐
10. You are good at **keeping secrets** and never **bear a grudge**.	☐	☐	☐	☐	☐
11. You find it hard to **keep your temper** if you think someone is **making a fool out of you**.	☐	☐	☐	☐	☐
12. You can be **brutally honest** and sometimes hurt others' feelings.	☐	☐	☐	☐	☐

Describe your personality and character using the phrases you've just learnt.

_____

_____

_____

Part 3 Lyrics for your reference

For the First Time
Kenny Loggins

Are those your eyes? Is that your smile?
I've been looking at you forever
But I never saw you before
Are these your hands holding mine?
Now I wonder how I could have been so blind

For the first time I am looking in your eyes
For the first time I'm seeing who you are
I can't believe how much I see
When you're looking back at me
Now I understand why love is...
Love is... for the first time...

Can this be real? Can this be true?
Am I the person I was this morning?
And are you the same you?
It's all so strange. How can it be
All along this love was right in front of me?

For the first time I am looking in your eyes
For the first time I'm seeing who you are
I can't believe how much I see
When you're looking back at me
Now I understand why love is...
Love is... for the first time...

Such a long time ago

I had given up on finding this emotion ever again

But you live with me now

Yes, I've found you somehow

And I've never been so sure

And for the first time I am looking in your eyes

For the first time I'm seeing who you are

Can't believe how much I see

When you're looking back at me

Now I understand why love is...

Love is...for the first time...

On My Own

Eponine

And now I'm all alone again

Nowhere to turn, no one to go to

Without a home, without a friend

Without a face to say hello to

And now the night is near

Now I can make believe he's here

Sometimes I walk alone at night

When everybody else is sleeping

I think of him and then I'm happy

With the company I'm keeping

The city goes to bed

And I can live inside my head

On my own

Pretending he's beside me

All alone

I walk with him till morning

Without him

I feel his arms around me

And when I lose my way I close my eyes

And he has found me

In the rain, the pavement shines like silver

All the lights are misty in the river

In the darkness, the trees are full of starlight

And all I see is him and me forever and forever

And I know it's only in my mind

That I'm talking to myself and not to him

And although I know that he is blind

Still I say, there's a way for us

I love him

But when the night is over

He is gone

The river's just a river

Without him

The world around me changes

The trees are bare and everywhere

The streets are full of strangers

I love him

But every day I'm learning

All my life

I've only been pretending

Without me

His world would go on turning

A world that's full of happiness

That I have never known

I love him

I love him

I love him

But only on my own

Part 4 My own dictionary

Look up in the dictionary

Use the first line for definitions, the second line for sentence examples.

1. make a decision   to decide

                                  E. g. My parents make the decisions in the family.

2. take responsibility for

3. get along with

4. get in touch with

5. make an appointment with

6. work sth. out

7. go through sth.

8. It won't be easy.

9. ups and downs

10. critically important

11. for the first time

12. at a loss for words

13. in command of the situation

14. on one's own

15. look sb. straight in the eye

16. keep looking

17. prefer to

18. react to

19. find a way

20. in return

21. crack a joke

22. clean up

23. turn to

24. phone up

25. tend to

26. at times

27. get on

28. as long as

29. in reality

30. instead of

31. get outside of yourself

32. for ages

33. What are you up to?

34. What are you doing around here?

35. Long time no see.

36. How are you doing?

37. Take care. / Mind how you go.

38. It's a pleasure talking to you.   _____

39. It was great speaking to you.   _____

                                          _____

Unit 2   Silver Linings

Part 1   Life problems

Write

You are going to watch a video about different problems. Try your best to write down as many of the problems as possible.

1. Uh, _____ are too high in NY.
2. Weather.
3. Money.
4. My problem? The tree.
5. 2—3 hours _____.
6. My daughter.
7. Parking tickets.
8. My 8 am class.
9. _____ in the cold.
10. Boyfriend problems _____.
11. Right now I think it's _____.
12. I hate long pants.
13. _____.
14. Sleep.
15. Student _____.
16. Ben Carson.
17. The person who _____ the pole in the _____.
18. Too many people _____.
19. My _____ a little too small.
20. I'm _____.

Unit 2 Silver linings

21. I don't like the cops.

22. I hate the smell... of pissy subways.

23. The Kardashians.

24. I can't have _____ ... that's my problem, hahaha.

25. My _____ girlfriend.

Part 2 How to make a suggestion

2.1 Listen

Listen to 5 ways of making a suggestion and write them down.

1. _____
2. _____
3. _____
4. _____
5. _____

2.2 Write

Put the following sentences into the correct column.

1. Can you give me a hand?

2. **I can't take it anymore.**

3. You look so sullen, anything wrong?

4. Is there anything wrong?

5. What's bothering you?

6. **What am I supposed to do?**

When you are having some problems, you can say:	When your friends are worried about you, they can say:

2.3 Work in pairs

Work with your partner. Take turns to use role cards A and B. Give yourself time to prepare for your role and think about the high frequency phrases you might use.

Role card A

You have the following problems with your study:

1. You'd like to read novels in English, but when you try you find them quite difficult and you get easily discouraged.

2. When you watch films in English you find it hard to understand the dialogue without **relying on** the subtitles.

3. Sometimes when you look words up in the dictionary you feel overwhelmed by all the different meanings and uses that are listed.

4. Your teacher told you that you should try to think in English, but you've no idea how to do it.

Talk to your partner for suggestions. You can decide to accept or reject it by saying:

Yes, that's a good idea.

That's easier said than done.

Role card B

Your partner is going to tell you about his or her problems with study. Give as many helpful suggestions as you can. When giving suggestions, you can say:

1. How about...?

2. Why don't you...?

3. Maybe you should...

4. I'd recommend...

5. Have you thought about...?

Unit 2 Silver linings

Part 3 Dear Abby

3.1 Read

Complete the sentences by matching column A with column B.

A	B
1. You should learn to	A. on the bright side of things.
2. I think you're	B. than peace of mind.
3. Young people develop self-esteem	C. for a reason.
4. Stop being	D. give yourself credit.
5. You should look	E. better off without him.
6. Bring it	F. such a baby.
7. Everything happens	G. on.
8. There is nothing more important	H. by doing volunteer job.
9. We'll cross that bridge	I. the bullet.
10. It's time to	J. when we come to it.
11. I would think twice	K. anything you want.
12. You can achieve	L. turn over a new leaf.
13. You need to bite	M. before taking the job.

3.2 Giving advice

What is your advice in the following situations? Write a response by using the high frequency collocations you have just learnt.

Dear Abby,

I am an 18-year-old girl who is happy, healthy and doing great in school. But lately I have felt sad, lonely and just plain frustrated. I used to talk to my parents about it, but I don't feel comfortable doing it anymore, and my friends don't like listening to me.

I have tried hard to **push back** these feelings, but it is **putting a strain** on me. Sometimes I **break down** crying and can't stop. Most people think it's just my age, but it's not. I want to talk to a psychologist, but I'm scared to ask for one. What am I **supposed to** do?

—Debbie

Dear Abby,

I'm 19, and for the last five months my family hasn't been getting along. We **act like** we love each other, but I'm not so sure. My mom and dad have been fighting.

I don't know if my parents are getting a divorce or not, but it's slowly **tearing my family apart**, and I don't know what to do. What can I do to keep my parents together?

—Calvin

Dear Abby,

I am so exhausted and have no time to spend with family and friends.

Every day I go to a lot of meetings and **take part in** after-school activities such as singing, dancing, and volunteer work. At night I want to sleep early, but some of my roommates are still playing computer games. I'm not free on weekends, because I have a part-time job at KFC.

I can't take it anymore. Please help.

—Ben

Dear Abby,

I find it difficult to **get down to work** in the evening and I can't concentrate on anything at the moment. I spend most of my time listening to records or playing the mobile phone instead of studying. The other students are much better than I am and I have difficulty in **keeping up with** them.

—George

3.3 Read

In the future, you are going to encounter a lot of problems in your job. How to solve these problems? Watch a video and get some ideas.

Most people only **pay attention to** the final product of a successful entrepreneur. They say things like "I can never be like them" or "They got lucky". What most don't see is what they overcome: all the struggles, daily rejections, the heartaches, the betrayals, the rumors, the criticism, the empty bank account, and all those lonely nights while trying to make their vision a reality. You see, the only difference between the one who quits and the one who doesn't is that they **showed up** every day. They worked hard every day. They hustled every day. They learned from proven mentors every day. They improved every day. They did all these, even when they felt like quitting every day. And eventually, they became who they are today.

3.4 Prepare for group work

What is your advice in the following situations? Write a response by using the high frequency phrases you have just learnt.

Dear Abby,

I've been **under stress** for some time at work. I have more responsibility and more work to do and it's becoming very hard to keep up. Some of my subordinates don't take things seriously. I'm more and more bad-tempered and it's starting to affect my home life: I've noticed that I'm often irritable with my wife and children. What's going wrong?

—David

Dear Abby,

I've just received an offer from another company. It's a better job—more responsibility and more money. The problem is that the company is more than two hours' drive away, so I'd be spending four hours a day travelling to and from work. Should I accept the job?

—Mike

Dear Abby,

I've been promoted within my department, and I'm now the boss of the people I used to work with. Most people are fine about this but a couple are very resentful. One person will not let me check any of his work: He sends it all directly to my boss before I can see it. Should I try to change his behavior?

—Mary

Dear Abby,

We are introducing a fully automated quality-checking procedure on the production line where I work. We are offering full training for staff to use the new systems. Though **in the long run**, we will need fewer people, we will not be firing anyone: we will reduce through natural wastage. **In spite of all this** the workers are strongly against the new procedures. What can I do to inspire confidence?

—Zoe

3.5 Write

Watch the video carefully and then complete the mentioned problems.

1. My sister has _____.
2. We _____ our home.

3. I cannot _____ for my family.

4. I lost my job _____ my medical condition.

5. I have been racially _____.

6. My doctor told me I _____ make it.

7. Teenage _____.

8. I can't _____ an education.

9. I was _____ at school.

10. I am a _____ mother.

11. My parents _____.

12. Anxiety _____ my life.

13. I have a problem with _____.

14. I lost my _____.

Part 4 Hand tracing

Draw a picture

Trace your hand on the paper and write down some problems you are experiencing now on the palm of your hand image.

Share your problems with your group members. Think about what you can do to manage your problems and write down your solutions on your "finger" image.

Part 5 Lyrics for your reference

After the Winter

Lenka

When the rain is **pouring down**

And there are snowflakes on your cheeks

When your heart is frozen over

And hasn't seen the sun in weeks

Just remember

Just remember

After the winter comes the spring

That's when the blue birds start to sing

And you can always **count on** this

After the winter comes the spring

When the trees have lost the color

And the sky is full of fears

When you feel you're **going under**

And your eyes are full of tears

When the bears are all in hiding

And you are hiding too

Oh, darling just remember

That everything will soon be new

Because after the winter comes the spring

That is when the blue birds start to use their wings

And you can always count on this

After the winter comes the spring

Just remember

Just remember

Just remember

Just remember

After the winter comes the spring

That's when the blue birds start to sing

And you can always count on this

After the winter comes the spring

After the winter comes the spring

These Times

SafetySuit

These times will try hard to define me

And I'll try to hold my head up high

But I've seen despair here from the inside

And it's got a one-track mind

And I have this feeling in my gut now

And I don't know what it is I'll find

Does anybody ever feel like

You're always one step behind?

Now I'm sitting alone here in my bed

I'm waiting for an answer I don't know that I'll get

I cannot stand to look in the mirror

I'm failing

I'm telling you these times are hard

But they will

And I know there's someone out there somewhere

Who has it much worse than I do

But I have a dream inside, a perfect life

I'd give anything just to work

It's like I'm only trying to dig my way out

Of all these thing I can't

And I am

Sitting alone here in my bed

I'm waiting for an answer I don't know that I'll get

I cannot stand to look in the mirror

I'm failing

I'm telling you these times are hard

But they will pass

They will pass

They will pass

These times are hard

But they will

These times will try hard to define me

But I will hold my head up high

Sitting alone here in my bed

I'm waiting for an answer I don't know that I'll get

I cannot stand to look in the mirror

I'm failing

I'm telling you these times are hard

But they will pass

And I know there's a reason

I just keep hoping it won't be long till I see it

And maybe if we throw up our hands and believe it

I'm telling you these times are hard

But they will pass

They will pass

They will pass

These times are hard

But they will pass

Part 6　My own dictionary

Look up in the dictionary

Use the first line for definitions, the second line for sentence examples.

1. How about...?

2. Why don't you...?

3. Maybe we should...

4. I'd recommend...

5. Have you thought about...?

6. rely on

7. That's easier said than done.

8. push back

9. break down

10. tear apart

11. keep up with

12. look on the bright side of things

13. be supposed to

14. There's nothing more important than peace of mind.

15. take part in

16. I can't take it anymore.

17. get down to work

18. Give yourself credit.

19. Give me a hand.

20. develop self-esteem

21. Bring it on.

22. Everything happens for a reason.

23. be better off

24. We'll cross the bridge when we come to it.

25. turn over a new leaf

26. Think twice before...

27. bite the bullet

28. in reality

29. pay attention to

30. show up

31. under stress

32. take sth. seriously

33. in the long run

34. in spite of all this

35. pick on

36. They will pass.

37. pour down

38. count on

39. go under

40. After the winter comes the spring.

Unit 3 Living in the Moment

Part 1 Happiness survey

1.1 Write

Overall, how happy would you say you are these days? Give your rating on a scale of 1(low) to 10(high). _____

What is happiness?

Take a moment to think about what happiness means to you. Note down whatever comes into your head.

What does happiness mean to you?
Example: A relaxing day at home with my family.

1.2 Read

Read the following sentences and try to use them to describe your present feelings about yourself.

1. I **feel particularly pleased** with the way I am.
2. I am intensely interested in other people.
3. I feel that **life is very rewarding.**
4. I have very warm feelings towards almost everyone.
5. I **am optimistic about** the future.
6. **I am always committed and involved.**
7. I think that the world is a good place.

8. I **am well satisfied about** everything in my life.

9. I always **have a cheerful effect on** others.

10. I feel that I am **in control of** my life.

11. I often **experience joy and elation.**

12. I find it easy to make decisions.

13. I feel I have **a great deal of energy.**

14. I usually **have a good influence on** events.

15. I have fun with other people.

___
___
___

Do you believe that making more money, new relationship, and winning the lottery will bring you happiness forever? According to the research, these things give only a temporary boost of happiness. How can we acquire sustained happiness? How can we build habits of happiness?

Part 2 Ways to be happier

2.1 Read

These pictures show the things that recent scientific research proved to have a positive impact on people's feelings of happiness and fulfillment. Work with your partner to categorize them into different ways to be happier.

Unit 3 Living in the Moment

3 EAT MORE FRUITS AND GREENY VEGETABLES.

4 DRINK GREEN TEA AND PLENTY OF WATER.

5 TRY TO MAKE AT LEAST THREE PEOPLE SMILE EACH DAY.

6 EAT BREAKFAST LIKE A KING, LUNCH LIKE A PRINCE AND DINNER LIKE A PAUPER.

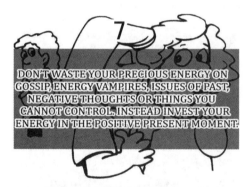
7 DON'T WASTE YOUR PRECIOUS ENERGY ON GOSSIP, ENERGY VAMPIRES, ISSUES OF PAST, NEGATIVE THOUGHTS OR THINGS YOU CANNOT CONTROL. INSTEAD INVEST YOUR ENERGY IN THE POSITIVE PRESENT MOMENT.

8 LIFE ISN'T FAIR, BUT IT'S STILL GOOD.

9 LIFE IS TOO SHORT TO WASTE TIME HATING ANYONE. FORGIVE THEM FOR EVERYTHING!

10 YOU DON'T HAVE TO WIN EVERY ARGUMENT. AGREE TO DISAGREE.

11. MAKE PEACE WITH YOUR PAST SO IT WON'T SPOIL THE PRESENT.

12. DON'T COMPARE YOURSELF TO OTHERS. COMPARE YOURSELF TO THE PERSON YOU WERE YESTERDAY.

13. NO ONE IS IN CHARGE OF YOUR HAPPINESS EXCEPT YOU.

14. HELP THE NEEDY, BE GENEROUS! BE A 'GIVER' NOT A 'TAKER'.

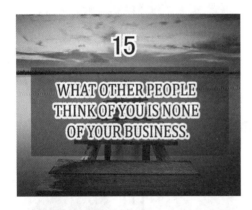

15. WHAT OTHER PEOPLE THINK OF YOU IS NONE OF YOUR BUSINESS.

16. TIME HEALS EVERYTHING.

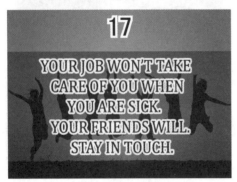

17. YOUR JOB WON'T TAKE CARE OF YOU WHEN YOU ARE SICK. YOUR FRIENDS WILL. STAY IN TOUCH.

18. HOWEVER GOOD OR BAD A SITUATION IS, IT WILL CHANGE.

Unit 3 Living in the Moment   31

2.2 Group work

Read the following sentences and tell whether they are positive(P), negative(N) or neutral(NL).

1) A friend **treated me to lunch.**

2) I beat my best friend at our favorite sport.

3) I didn't have enough money to buy a new T-shirt.

4) I felt like I had **too many responsibilities.**

5) I finished a project **ahead of time.**

6) I forgot my computer password.

7) I found gum stuck at the bottom of my shoes.

8) I found something I really wanted on sale.

9) I found something I thought I had lost.

10) I got a hug.

11) I had to **wait in line** at a store or dining hall.

12) I misplaced or lost something unimportant.

13) I saw a great movie.

14) I spend **quality time** with my pet.

15) I spilled something on my clothes.

16) I started a new hobby.

17) My dormmates are noisy.

18) **Unexpected weather** hit my town.

2.3 Write

Happy/ Unhappy Lists: What makes you happy or unhappy? Write them below.

Happy	Unhappy

2.4 Write

Complete the following sentences.

- Although _____,

    I'm still thankful because _____.

- Although _____,

    I'm still thankful because _____.

- Although _____,

    I'm still thankful because _____.

- Although _____,

    I'm still thankful because _____.

2.5 Watch

Watch a video and pay attention to the following sentences.

a. I wanna thank the 1. _____ for honoring *Whiplash* with this 2. _____.

b. **I couldn't have done this without** 3. _____.

c. I wanna thank you 4. **from the bottom of my heart** for 5. _____

d. I will forever 6. _____, your art changed my life.

2.6 Write

Make your own "Thank you speech".

_____
_____
_____
_____

2.7 Watch

Watch a video about Essena O'Neill. Are you **for or against** social media? You will be assigned by your teacher to debate on this issue.

One of the most popular IG models in the world quit social media **for good** and you won't believe her reason why!!

Hey guys, it's Emily for HollywoodLife. com. Okay, we all know the **downsides of social media**: the stuff you post isn't exactly your real life. Let's be honest. I've done it. This selfie... it actually is one of 30. Well, that's exactly what's started to get 19 year old Australian model Essena O'Neil.

Essena has over 800,000 Instagram followers but now she says she **is done with** all social media stuff for good. She admitted in a really emotional 17-minute Youtube video on her very popular channel btw that **getting attention** from strangers is not a real life experience and certainly has not made her happy...

(Essena:) And I'm quitting social media to tell anyone, everyone who's still watching, that I was miserable. I had it all, and I was miserable because when you let yourself **be defined** by numbers, you let yourself be defined by something that is not pure, that is not real, and that is not love.

Essena has now deleted over 2,000 photos from her feed that she felt were merely self-promotional and also changed the captions of her former photos that once idealized her perfect body and perfect life. Like this one she edited to experience her real feelings: *Took over 100 in similar poses trying to make my stomach look good. Would have hardly eaten all day. Would have yelled at my little sister to keep taking them until I* **was somewhat proud of** *this. Yep so totally #goals.*

Wow. But one of the saddest part about all this is that Essena's whole career has **let down** the real person she was at 12 years old before all this started.

(Essena:) At 12, I thought I was nothing. And then here at 19, with all these followers, I don't even know what is real and what is not, because I let myself be defined by something that is so not real. Being with people in your real life, hugging people, talking to people, going out in the park, into nature, that is fucking real life!! And I didn't do it for the **majority of my life** because I was just living in a screen, wishing that people will value me, that people would hear me, that people would just know me. And that's all I thought I should do. And it's not real!

I have to say I have so much respect for her honesty and bravery. Essena, we love you and this is so inspiring. So I wanna hear from you guys, would you ever be able to give up your social media?

2.8 Write

Watch a video and summarize the ideas in your own words.

_____
_____
_____

2.9 Prepare for group work

Answer the following questions and share your answers in a group.

1) How would your friends describe you? _____

2) How would your parents describe you? _____

3) How would your teacher describe you? _____

4) How would you describe yourself? _____

The Best of Me

_____

_____

_____

2.10 Read

To Risk

William Arthur Word

To laugh is to risk appearing a fool.

To weep is to risk appearing sentimental.

To **reach out** to another is to risk involvement.

To expose feelings is to risk exposing your true self.

To place your ideas and dreams **before a crowd** is to risk their loss.

To love is to risk not being loved **in return**.

To live is to **risk dying**.

To hope is to risk despair.

To try is to risk failure.

But risks must be taken because **the greatest hazard** in life is **to risk nothing**.

The person who risks nothing, does nothing, has nothing, is nothing.

He may avoid **suffering and sorrow**,

But he cannot learn, feel, change, grow or live.

Chained by his servitude he is a slave who has forfeited all freedom.

Only a person who risks is free.

The pessimist complains about the wind;

The optimist expects it to change;

And the realist adjusts the sails.

Do you like taking risks or do you prefer to play it safe? Answer these five questions to find out your attitude toward taking risks.

Are you a risk taker?

1) In an exam of 6 topics where only 2 will appear, what do you do?

   a) Study all 6, just **in case**.

   b) Study 4 of them. **Chances are that** 2 will be in the exam.

   c) Study 2 and **cross your fingers**!

2) What would you prefer to do at the weekend?

   a) Stay at home.

   b) Go hiking around a nearby village.

   c) Do **extreme sports**, like rock climbing or mountain biking.

3) Would you like to do a bungee jump?

   a) No way! Not for all the money in the world.

   b) Maybe, if there was a low bridge with deep water underneath.

   c) Any time. That's what bridges are for!

4) When you cross the road, what do you do?

   a) Always go to the traffic lights and wait for the green man.

   b) Find a safe place to cross and look both ways.

   c) Cross anywhere. Cars will stop for me!

5) Imagine you win some money in a lottery. What do you do with it?

   a) **Put it in the bank**-you may really need it one day.

   b) Spend it all.

   c) Use it to bet again.

Now count the number of As, Bs and Cs you put and read the results:

- Mostly As-You like to play it safe and hate taking risks.

- Mostly Bs-You take risks from time to time but are quite sensible.

- Mostly Cs-You like to live life on the edge! Take care!

2.11 Write

Watch a video and figure out the implied meaning of "shoes".

_____

2.12 Write

Write your own "To risk" poem.

To _____ is to risk _____ .

To _____ is to risk _____ .

To _____ is to risk _____ .

But risks must be taken because _____

_____

2.13 Read

What's the best thing that someone has done for you? How did it make you feel?

What's the best thing that you have done for another person? Read the following sentences.

1. Give up your seat.

2. Hold a door open for someone.

3. **Give a(sincere)compliment.**

4. Make someone laugh.

5. Give someone a hug.

6. Take time to really listen to someone.

7. Make someone new feel welcome.

8. Give directions to someone who's lost.

9. Have a conversation with a stranger.

10. **Pick up litter** as you walk.

11. Let someone in front of you in the supermarket queue.

12. Tell someone they **mean a lot** to you.

13. Read a story with a child.

14. Offer your change to someone struggling to find the right amount.

15. Buy cakes or fruit for your friends.

16. Tell someone if you notice they're doing a good job.

17. Pass on a book you've enjoyed.

18. Say sorry to someone.

19. Forgive someone for what they've done.

20. Visit a sick friend, relative or neighbor.

21. Buy an **unexpected gift** for someone.

22. Do a chore that you don't normally do.

23. Help out someone in need.

24. Donate your old things to charity.

25. Visit someone who may be lonely.

26. Give blood.

27. Get back in contact with someone you've lost touch with.

28. Organize a fundraising event.

29. Volunteer your time for a charity.

30. Plan a party.

2.14 Write

This week, what kind thing do you intend to do for:

A. your roommates _____

B. familiar strangers _____

C. best friends _____

D. family members _____

E. others _____

Part 3 Scripts for your reference

1

Wow. I want to thank the Academy for honoring *Whiplash* with this award. I couldn't have done this without the contributions of the entire cast and crew of *Whiplash*, Blumhouse, Bold Films, Right of Way Films, our amazing team at Sony Pictures Classics, Michael Barker, and Tom Bernard, and our team at WME. Also my assistant editors John To and Eugene Lok, I couldn't have done it without you guys. Miles Teller and J. K. Simmons, I need to thank you for delivering gold to the cutting room every day. And most of all, I need to thank the person who never once threw a chair at my head but always pushed to make it better, the writer and director, Damien Chazelle. Damien, I want to thank you from the bottom of my heart for sharing this journey with me. I... I will forever be indebted to you. Your art changed my life. And to Lah Cross and Jim Cross, my mother and father, and my beautiful wife Holly, and my children Nova and Peri, you made my life! Thank you so much.

2

When I was 16 years old, I tried to kill myself, because I felt weird, and I felt different, and I felt like I did not belong. And now I'm standing here, and I would like for this moment to be for that kid out there who feels like she's weird or she's different or she doesn't fit in anywhere. Yes, you do. I promise you do. Stay weird, stay different, and then when it's your turn, and you are standing on this stage, please pass the message to the next person who comes along.

3

Big Fish (2003)

Young man: I have to leave. Tonight.

Old man: Why?

Young man: This town is more than any man could ask for. And if I were to **end up** here, I would consider myself lucky. But the truth is, I'm just not ready to **end up**

anywhere.

Old man: But no one's ever left.

Girl: How are you gonna make it without your shoes?

Young man: Well, I suspect it will hurt. A lot. Now, I'm sorry, but... Well, goodbye.

Old man: You won't find a better place.

Young man: I don't expect to.

Girl: Promise me you'll come back.

Young man: I promise. Someday. When I'm really **supposed to**.

Part 4 My own dictionary

Look up in the dictionary

Use the first line for definitions, the second line for sentence examples.

1. a great deal of energy

2. ahead of time

3. be committed and involved

4. be defined

5. be done with

6. be grateful/thankful

7. be indebted to

8. be intensely interested in

Unit 3 Living in the Moment

9. be optimistic about

10. be somewhat proud of

11. be well satisfied about

12. Chances are that...

13. come into one's head

14. couldn't have done this without

15. cross your fingers

16. doesn't fit anywhere

17. downsides of social media

18. end up

19. experience joy and elation

20. extreme sports

21. feel particularly pleased

22. feel weird

23. for good

24. from the bottom of my heart

25. get attention

26. give a (sincere) compliment

27. have a cheerful effect on

28. have a good influence on

29. have very warm feelings

30. in case

31. in control of

32. Life is very rewarding.

33. majority of someone's life

34. mean a lot

35. pick up litter

36. put it in the bank

37. quality time

38. stay weird

Unit 3 Living in the Moment   43

39. suffering and sorrow

40. supposed to

41. the greatest hazard

42. to risk nothing

43. too many responsibilities

44. treat somebody to lunch

45. unexpected gift

46. unexpected weather

47. wait in line

Unit 4　Wanderlust

Part 1　Dream destinations

1.1　Speak

Your teacher will show you some pictures of famous tourist destinations. Watch carefully and shout loudly the first word or description that comes to your mind and guess which tourist destination it is. You may refer to the following words and descriptions.

Places		Description
SHENZHEN	VIENNA	relaxing atmosphere great for couples
BEIJING	TOKYO	good for shopping very impressive hot springs
DAMEISHA	AMSTERDAM	**plenty of fresh air** perfect for families
TIBET	SHANGHAI	great scenery skyscraper open spaces
OXFORD	ROME	**too crowded** extremely noisy
DISNEYLAND	SEOUL	hospitable locals lots of history
TAJ MAHAL	KUALA	great for swimming **see the wildlife**
HUIZHOU	LUMPUR	an educational experience great for sailing
NEW YORK	DUBAI	magnificent view **really fascinating** tourist attraction
HONG KONG	ISTANBUL	great weather see the sights to experience the culture
PARIS	SINGAPORE	romantic expensive/pricey/over-priced
LONDON	YELLOW STONE	spectacular views breathtaking scenery
TAIPEI	RUSSIA	secluded beach peaceful/tranquil countryside
EGYPT	AUSTRALIA	be well worth seeing tree-lined avenues
MALDIVES	BANGKOK	with lively bars and fashionable clubs
LOS ANGELES		heavy traffic run-down buildings
		urban wasteland comfortable suburbs
		great for singles/ kids/ seniors

1.2 Watch

Watch a video about top travel destinations.

1. South Africa

I think the great thing about South Africa... there was once a phrase termed a "world in one country". And **in many ways** it does deliver on that promise. The ability to see wildlife in its natural habitat, up close and personal and **in very authentic way**, is very true. South Africa has a **tremendous warmth** to its people. They embrace you in their cultures. They are great cultural experiences. And it really delivers from a food and wine perspective which is a little-known aspect of the country. **Absolutely world-class.**

2. Argentina

What makes Argentina a special destination is, I say, a big country. It has **all types of** different climates and tourist attractions. And it's good to travel to Argentina **all year long**. We have in the north, this semi-tropical climate and you can visit the Iguazu Falls. In the mountain, we have the wine region of Argentina in the south Patagonia, so **you have many options**. And of course, Buenos Aires, which is the capital. Buenos Aires has always all kinds of celebrations so it's always a good time to go.

3. Philippines

It's more fun in the Philippines. Even(with) the people, you can talk to(easily). You can make friends with them. You can travel with them and they can even invite you in their homes when you visit the country. So number one, the people. We are the third largest(English) speaking nation in the world. And secondly, adventure. We can do **a lot of activities** in the Philippines, from surfing, diving, wakeboarding, whitewater rafting. **So name it**, we have it for adventure. And the beach also.

4. Czech Republic

Czech Republic is located in Central Europe, so it can be visited as a single destination, but it can also **combine with** other destinations with neighboring countries and I think this is great. It's a small country so you can spend about a week there and you can pretty much see the whole country which is great as well. We have twelve world heritage sites. We have over 2,000 castles and chateaux which is the highest number in the world actually for a square kilometer. So it's the culture, architecture and the history, certainly.

5. Tahiti

You know I think everybody sees this stunning gorgeous pictures of overwater bungalows and lagoons, but honestly most people even say **those pictures do not even do justice.** You are there and you pinch yourself (because) you can't believe the **shades of color.** Each lagoon is clearer, more blue, more beautiful than the next and it's really like no place on earth. I've personally been to 60 countries and I can tell you that **the beauty is unsurpassed.**

Describe your dream destination using the phrases you've just learnt. Let your classmate guess what or where it is.

_____
_____
_____
_____

Part 2　Agreeing and disagreeing

2.1　Write

There are different ways of expressing agreement and disagreement, such as **"You're right there", "Definitely", "You must be joking", "I don't agree at all". Listen to an audio clip and take notes.**

agreement	disagreement

2.2 Read

Rearrange the dialogue.

1. A: Travelling at this time will wear both of us out.

2. **B: It's long been my dream** to go to Seoul.

3. A: **I'm up for** visiting our relatives in Guangzhou.

4. A: What's your plan for this holiday?

5. **B:** But we always go to Guangzhou on vacation. I really want to **make a change.**

6. **B:** Do you really think so?

7. **B:** I don't mind as long as I can see Bigbang, Girl's Generation and Super Junior.

8. A: I am not so sure about that. **Maybe it's better to** have a staycation.

Correct order: _____

2.3 Work in pairs

Choose your dream destination and discuss with your partner. If your partner shares the same place with you, try to agree with him/her. If your partner's dream destination is different from you, try to disagree with him/her and persuade him/her to go with you.

Part 3   Let's go!

3.1 Write

Gap-filling.

M: What are you looking at?

F: Tours for our vacation. I was thinking that it'll be hard for us to _____ on our own, so I think joining a tour is a good idea.

M: Really, I thought we'd _____ leisurely to _____. I don't like the _____ of tours. I'd rather have the time to _____ each sight. Not _____ just to say I've been there.

F: Tours _____. I'm sure we can find one that isn't too fast-paced or strenuous for you.

M: And I don't want to eat all my meals with the tour group. I want some time to explore on our own.

F: All right, I'm looking at a tour that has the perfect itinerary. It's also gotten _____. It includes a tour guide, all admission fees, accommodations, ground transportation and most of the meals. And there are several free mornings and afternoons _____, so we can explore on our own.

M: I don't know.

F: The _____ is for you to plan each stop of our trip.

M: A tour is sounding better and better.

3.2 Prepare for group work

As you know the difference between a holiday package and a non-organized tour, express your point of view to your partner and figure out whether he/she agrees with you or not.

3.3 Write

Dictation: Bad travelling experience.

1.
2.
3.
4.
5.
6.
7.
8.
9.
10.

Share your travelling experience (good or bad) with your group members.

Homework: Design an e-postcard.

Part 4   My own dictionary

Look up in the dictionary

Use the first line for definitions, the second line for sentence examples.

1. relaxing atmosphere

2. great for couples

3. good for shopping

4. hot springs

5. plenty of fresh air

6. perfect for families

7. great scenery

8. open spaces

9. too crowded

10. extremely noisy

11. lots of history

12. hospitable locals

13. great for swimming

14. see the wildlife

15. an educational experience

16. great for sailing

17. magnificent view

18. tourist attraction

19. great weather

20. spectacular view

21. to experience the culture

22. breathtaking scenery

23. be well worth seeing

24. tree-lined avenues

25. lively bars and fashionable clubs

26. heavy traffic

27. run-down buildings

28. urban wasteland

29. comfortable suburbs

Unit 4　Wanderlust

30. great for singles/ kids/ seniors

31. That's for sure.

32. I agree 100%.

33. I couldn't agree with you more.

34. That's exactly what I think.

35. That's exactly how I feel.

36. Tell me about it!

37. You're telling me!

38. I'll say!

39. I suppose so.

40. You must be joking!

41. It's long been my dream.

42. I'm up for...

43. make a change

44. Maybe it's better to...

45. get around

46. make our way around

47. fast pace

48. come in all shapes and sizes

49. rave reviews

50. built in

51. jet-lagged

52. a seedy area

53. tourist trap

Unit 5　Shopping Season

Part 1　Luxury or bargain?

1.1　Speak

Watch a video clip and answer the following questions.

1. What does the heroine think of Mom's price shoes?

2. What kind of shoes does the heroine prefer?

3. What kind of shoes would you like to buy? (shoes with discount or original price shoes)

1.2　Write

Listen to an audio clip and take notes.

1. _____
2. _____
3. _____
4. _____
5. _____
6. _____
7. _____
8. _____
9. _____
10. _____

1.3　Work in pairs

Describe what your partner is wearing or holding by using the phrases you have just learnt.

Part 2 How do you spend your money?

2.1 Write

Listen to an audio clip and fill in the blanks by using the phrases in the box.

worth the wait	clipping coupons	cut corners
keep track of	putting me on	mess around
penny pincher	rebate offers	great offer

M: What are you doing? 1. _____. That's a waste of time.

F: You can think what you like, but these days we have to 2. _____ wherever we can.

M: No one actually save much money using coupons.

F: That's what you think. The last time I went to the grocery store, I saved over twenty dollars just by using coupons.

M: How can you 3. _____ all of the expiration dates and the terms and conditions? It's not worth the trouble.

F: Do you feel that way about 4. _____ too? A month ago, I bought our new TV and saved twenty percent. And yesterday I bought a pack of DVDs for just two dollars.

M: Are you 5. _____? A pack of DVDs for two dollars?

F: Yes, it was a 6. _____. But it was only for one day. I had to cut out the UPC code, **fill out** a form, and mail it in with a receipt to the manufacturer. Then I sent the copy of the receipt to the retailer and got another discount. That's how I got the DVDs **for next to nothing**.

M: You might save money with rebates. But you have to **sit around** forever waiting for the rebate check.

F: It's true that the turn-around is often 8—10 weeks, but some of the offers are 7. _____

M: Do what you like. But I'm too busy to 8. _____ with coupons and rebates.

F: That's why you married a 9. _____. **If I left it up to you**, we'd be in the poor house by now.

2.2 Read

How do you spend your money?

1. Where would you choose to go for your summer holiday?

    a. somewhere special-regardless of the cost

    b. somewhere you think will be nice, but not too expensive

    c. a camping trip

2. If you're handed a foreign coin in your change, what do you do?

    a. throw it away

    b. pass it on to someone else

    c. look for a slot machine that will accept it

3. If you saw a wallet stuffed with money lying in the gutter and there was nobody around, what would you do?

    a. take it to the nearest police station

    b. spend the money as quickly as possible

    c. ignore it and keep walking

4. What gift would you give your potential mother-in-law who doesn't approve of you?

    a. a present which you received but don't want

    b. something very expensive as a peace offering

    c. something safe like a box of chocolates

5. When do you buy new clothes?

    a. whenever you feel like it

    b. only when you need something

    c. just to cheer yourself up

6. What would you do if you unexpectedly came into some money?

    a. save half and spend the rest of it on presents

b. invest it

c. spend the lot in one glorious **shopping spree**

7. How much are you willing to give to charity?

    a. nothing

    b. 10% or more of your monthly allowance

    c. it depends, but less than you spend on new clothes

8. If you were planning a celebration party, what would it be?

    a. an extravagant affair with sophisticated entertainment

    b. something out of the ordinary

    c. a quiet affair somewhere local

9. You put a friend up for a couple of weeks, but he/she offers nothing towards food. What would your reaction be?

    a. not to expect anything

    b. ask for the amount that you think you're owed

    c. resolve never to invite that person again

10. What presents can your friends expect from you?

    a. more expensive than you can really afford

    b. promises of wonderful presents which never materialize

    c. inexpensive but carefully chosen ones

KEYs

1. a-3 b-2 c-1   6. a-2 b-1 c-3

2. a-4 b-2 c-1   7. a-0 b-3 c-1

3. a-1 b-5 c-2   8. a-3 b-2 c-1

4. a-1 b-3 c-2   9. a-3 b-1 c-2

5. a-3 b-1 c-2   10. a-3 b-0 c-2

WHAT YOUR SCORE MEANS

26-33   **Money burns a hole in your pocket!** You need to be more responsible with how you get and use it.

15-25 Money is something that never worries you too much. You enjoy having it, and the chance to be generous, but relationships **take priority**.

0-14 You are very cautious with money. Reconsider your attitudes or you may be seen as a miser.

2.3 Work in pairs

In pairs, complete the sentences below with the following words.

easy   made   mouth   rainy   trees   water

1. Paul must be _____ of money. Look at his brand new sports car!
2. You keep saying you can beat me. Why don't you put your money where your _____ is?
3. Don't be so wasteful! Money doesn't grow on _____, you know.
4. Save some money for a _____ day. Don't spend it all at once.
5. Some people think running website is _____ money.
6. Julia spends money like _____. She goes shopping almost everyday.

2.4 Prepare for group work

Ask a list of questions to find out your classmate's spending habits.

Part 3 Gift certificate or coupon

3.1 Write

Running dictation.

1. _____
2. _____
3. _____
4. _____
5. _____
6. _____

7. _____
8. _____
9. _____
10. _____
11. _____
12. _____
13. _____
14. _____
15. _____

Like	Dislike	Giving advice

3.2 Prepare for group work

Good news! Rainbow Department Store is celebrating their 30th anniversary and they are giving away gift certificates for every **group** in our class. You can buy anything at the shop for as long as the total doesn't exceed ￥10,000. Make your shopping list below. Discuss with your group members by using the phrases you've learnt.

Items	Price

Oops! Rainbow Department Store makes a new requirement. You can't buy things for yourself. You can only buy gifts for your family members and friends. You will have a budget of ￥100 for each person. First, think about the following questions:

1. What does this person like to do?

2. What sort of thing would this person like?

3. List some gifts they would like:_____

Then, finish the following table and discuss with your partner to choose the best gift for your beloved ones.

Items(for whom)	Reasons to buy	Price

3.3 Write

Finding a perfect gift.

work yourself up	hold it against me	pick out
get carried away	put any thought into	racking my brain
boggles my mind	knock her socks off	one piece of advice

F: Help! I still need to buy a gift for my mother and I can't seem to think of the perfect present—something that'll really 1._____

M: Why don't you just get her a gift certificate or a gift card? That way, she can 2._____ her own gift.

F: Oh, she would hate that. She would think that I didn't 3._____ buying her a present at all, while I've been 4._____ to think of something she'll like. Maybe I should buy her a car.

M: Now, don't 5._____ You get like this every year. I know you want to please your mother, but remember—it's the thought that counts.

F: I wish that were true. If I get her the wrong gift, I'm afraid she will be disappointed or worse, she'll 6._____ for the rest of my life.

M: It 7. _____ how you can 8. _____ like this every year.

F: How can I not? You know my mother.

M: Yes, I do. And I have 9. _____ for you: buy her a gift she can return.

Part 4 My own dictionary

Look up in the dictionary

Use the first line for definitions, the second line for sentence examples.

1. It cost a fortune.
   _____
   _____

2. It cost an arm and a leg.
   _____
   _____

3. That's a rip-off.
   _____
   _____

4. It was a real bargain.
   _____
   _____

5. dirt cheap
   _____
   _____

6. cut corners
   _____
   _____

7. keep track of
   _____
   _____

8. put somebody on
   _____
   _____

9. mess around
   _____
   _____

10. penny pincher
    _____
    _____

11. great offer
    _____
    _____

12. regardless of

13. approve of

14. It depends.

15. Money burns a hole in your pocket !

16. take priority

17. It fits me well.

18. It is worth every penny.

19. in favor of

20. I'm fed up with...

21. If I were you...

22. You might as well...

23. fill out

24. for next to nothing

25. shopping spree

26. take priority

27. knock somebody's socks off

28. pick out

29. put any thought into

30. to rack one's brains

31. get carried away

32. hold it against somebody

33. boggle one's mind

34. work up

35. one piece of advice

36. be made of money

37. Put your money where your mouth is.

38. save money for a rainy day

39. spend money like water

40. easy money

41. Money doesn't grow on trees.

Unit 6 A New Me

Part 1 New Year's resolution

1.1 Write

Fill in the blanks.

This is the time of year when people make their New Year's resolutions. At the beginning of a new year, people 1. _____ of their lives and decide to make some changes. A lot of people want to 2. _____. They 3. _____ go to the 4. _____ and 5. _____ every day. Many people also decide to 6. _____. After over-indulging at holiday meals, people feel the need to 7. _____ and 8. _____. Many people also promise to 9. _____ smoking or drinking and 10. _____. Whatever resolution you make, don't forget the most important one: promise not to have to make the same resolution next year.

1.2 Work in pairs

Watch a video and tell your partner what is the heroine's New Year's resolutions.

_____

_____

1.3 Write

Find the resolutions that go together and place them under the correct heading.

Personality development	Career and finance	Health	Society

1.4 Read

Read the following list of others' resolutions and take the previous resolutions into consideration. Pick five in your mind and describe it to your group members without saying the exact words. E.g. I want to improve my self image by curling my hair. It means "change my hair style"(number 5). Your classmate will guess.

1) stop buying clothes

2) quit smoking or smoke way less

3) lose 5 kilos

4) volunteer to help others

5) change my hair style

6) take a trip

7) save money

8) make more money

9) study harder

10) learn something new every day

11) make my parents proud

Unit 6 A New Me

12) find Mr. / Miss Right

13) be popular

14) be productive

15) be more positive

1.5 Speak

Look at the pictures on Powerpoint and decide which resolution people could make to improve their life. You can also make up your own.

Part 2　Keep your New Year's resolution

2.1 Write

Watch a video clip and write down the tips.

- 1. _____ early: write down your resolutions.
- Be 2. _____: a lot more 3. _____.
- Keep a 4. _____ attitude.
- 5. _____ your resolutions; 6. _____ one and 7. _____ with it.
- 8. _____ yourself.

2.2 Speak

Watch the video between father and son and answer the following questions.

- What's the boy's dream?
- How does the father feel about it?
- How did the boy feel at the end?
- Watch the video clip again and figure out the meaning of the following words.

go pro: _____

below (above) average: _____

probably: _____

ultimately: _____

rank: _____

somewhere around there: _____

excel at: _____

- If you were the boy's father, write a note to the son to encourage him.

_____

_____

_____

2.3 Write

Watch a video clip and write down the tips.

- Specific tips

Plan 1. _____ : start to get things ready now.

Set realistic goals: 2. _____, realistic, 3. _____ with a time frame.

Have a 4. _____ plan; if you lose 5. _____ don't mean you fail 6. _____, get back on that horse, make a new 7. _____.

2.4 Work in pairs

We hope all of you **feel pumped up**. Summarize the tips to keep New Year's resolutions according to your own experience and the previous videos.

1) _____

2) _____

3) _____

4) _____

5) _____

6) _____

7) _____

8) _____

Part 3　Your New Year's resolution

3.1　Write

Write down your New Year's resolution.

_____

_____

_____

3.2　Work in pairs

Talk about New Year's resolutions by asking the following questions.

1) What do you need to do to reach your goal?

2) What sacrifices are you willing to make?

3) On a scale of 1—10, how strong is your desire to achieve your goal?

4) What are the benefits of reaching your goal?

5) How will you encourage yourself when you want to give up?

6) What will you say to people who tell you that you can't reach your goal?

7) How can friends and family members help you achieve your goal?

8) Is there a local support group that you can join to help you achieve your goal?

Everybody takes turns to comment on other's New Year's resolutions by using the following highlighted expressions.

1) When you are talking about your New Year's resolutions, you can use the following expressions:

I am going to **talk a little bit about** how to lose 5 pounds in a month.

To tell you a secret, I can't stop biting my nails.

To tell you the truth, I hate my hairstyle and I want to change it.

2) When you want to show your determination, you can use the following expressions:

I swear.

Why would I lie?

Cross my heart and hope to die.

3) When you want to show your agreement, you can use the following expressions:

Needless to say, belly dancing makes girls hot.

It goes without saying that every child wants to make his / her parents proud.

Generally speaking, finding Mr. Right is not easy.

4) When you want to encourage somebody, you can use the following expressions:

Go on, you can do it.

I **have faith in** you.

I **have confidence in** you.

I trust you completely.

Let me know if there's anything I can do.

5) When you want to express doubt or caution, you can use the following expressions:

Is that all?

That won't do.

One step at a time.

I didn't get it.

I find that hard to believe.

6) When you want to give some advice, you can use the following expressions:

You should...

Why don't you...

You'd better do...

Homework

Write down your New Year's resolution while considering your classmate's advice. Send it to your future self by e-mail.

Part 4 Scripts for your reference

Bridget Jones's Diary (2001)

Scene 1

Bridget: It all began on New Year's Day... in my 32nd year of being single. Once again I found myself on my own... and going to my mother's annual "Turkey Curry" buffet. Every year she tries to fix me up with some bushy-haired, middle-aged bore... and I feared this year would be no exception.

Mom: There you are, dumpling.

Bridget: My mum, a strange creature...

Mom: By the way, the Darcys are here. They brought Mark with them.

Bridget: Ah, here we go.

Mom: You remember Mark. You used to play in his paddling pool. He's a barrister, very well-off.

Bridget: No, I don't remember.

Mom: He's divorced, apparently. His wife was Japanese. Very cruel race. Now, what are you going to put on?

Bridget: This.

Mom: Don't be silly, Bridget. You'll never get a boyfriend if you look like you've wandered out of Auschwitz. Run upstairs. Laid out something lovely on your bed....

Scene 2

Bridget: Great. I was wearing a carpet. Maybe this was the mysterious Mr. Right... I'd been waiting my whole life to meet. Maybe not.

Mom: She used to run around your lawn with no clothes on, remember?

Darcy: No, not as such.

Bridget: So.

Darcy: So.

Bridget: Are you staying at your parents' for New Year?

Darcy: Yes. You?

Bridget: Oh, no, no. I was in London at a party last night... so I'm afraid I'm a bit hung-over. Wish I could be lying with my head in a toilet like all normal people. New Year's resolution: Drink less. Oh, and quit smoking. And keep New Year's resolutions. And stop talking total nonsense to strangers. In fact, stop talking full stop.

Darcy: Yes, well, perhaps it's time to eat. (**speaking to his mother**) Mother, I do not need a blind date. Particularly not with some verbally incontinent spinster... who smokes like a chimney, drinks like a fish and dresses like her mother.

Bridget: Yummy. Turkey curry. My favorite. And that was it. Right there. Right there. That was the moment. I suddenly realized that unless something changed soon... I was going to live a life where my major relationship... was with a bottle of wine... and I'd finally die fat and alone...

The Pursuit of Happyness (2006)

Christopher: Hey, Dad. I'm going pro.

Christopher Gardner: Okay. Yeah, I don't know, you know. You'll probably be about as good as I was. That's kind of the way it works, you know. I was below average. You know, so you'll probably ultimately rank... somewhere around there, you know, so... I really... You'll excel at a lot of things, just not this. I don't want you shooting this ball all day and night. All right?

Christopher: All right. Okay.

Christopher Gardner: All right, go ahead.

Christopher Gardner: Hey. Don't ever let somebody tell you... you can't do something. Not even me. All right?

Christopher: All right.

Christopher Gardner: You got a dream... you gotta protect it. People can't do something themselves... they wanna tell you you can't do it. If you want something, go get it. Period. Let's go.

Part 5 My own dictionary

Look up in the dictionary

Use the first line for definitions, the second line for sentence examples.

1. above average _____
_____

2. acquire a better job _____
_____

3. all day and night _____
_____

4. balance my budget _____
_____

5. balance work and family _____
_____

6. be pumped up _____
_____

7. become financially independent

8. become fit

9. below average

10. blind date

11. control debt

12. Cross my heart and hope to die.

13. excel at

14. fix sb. up

15. generally speaking

16. get fit

17. get into shape

18. get involved in community

19. get stressed out

20. go get it

21. go green

Unit 6 A New Me

22. go on a diet

23. go pro

24. have confidence in

25. have faith in

26. Have you ever...

27. health club

28. hung over

29. I swear.

30. I'd been waiting...

31. improve self-image

32. Is that all?

33. It goes without saying that...

34. keep a positive attitude

35. keep a record

36. laugh more

37. Let me know...

38. lose weight

39. make a commitment

40. Needless to say...

41. not even sb.

42. overwhelm with

43. quit smoking

44. reduce stress

45. reward yourself

46. smoke way less

47. volunteer to help others

48. vow to

49. Why don't you...?

50. Why would I lie?

51. I wish I could...

52. work out

53. work smarter

54. You should...

55. You'd better...

Unit 7　Life Is a Hobby

Part 1　What do you have in common?

1.1　Speak

Look at the pictures and **figure out** what kind of hobbies they are.

1.2　Work in pairs

Talk with your partner about your common hobbies and fill out the following Venn diagram.

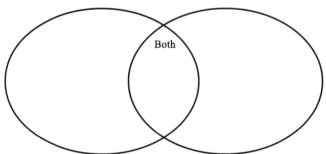

1.3 Prepare for group work

Complete each of the following sentences with T/F information about yourself. Let your classmate guess which ones are true and which are false.

1. I often play...

2. I sometimes go...

3. I... after school/ dinner

4. I can... very well.

5. On Sundays, I usually...

6. I feel best when...

7. I find it easy to...

1.4 Write

Watch a video and take notes on the important phrases and sentences.

_____

_____

_____

1.5 Speak

Ask your partner the following questions.

1) What do you do in your free time?

2) What is your number one hobby?

3) How much time do you usually spend on your hobbies?

4) What do your hobbies say about you?

5) Are your hobbies expensive?

6) Can you **make money** from doing your hobby?

7) How long have you had this hobby?

8) Does your hobby interfere with your work or personal life?

9) Does your hobby influence your choice of friends?

10) What are the strangest hobbies you have heard of?

Language Bank

1) I like climbing mountains.

2) **I'm fond of** listening to music.

3) **I'm crazy about** dance.

4) **I'm wild about** cars.

5) **I'm into** collecting stamps.

6) **I take a great interest** in sports.

7) I enjoy drinking beer in the summer.

8) I like yoga.

9) I do aerobics once a week.

10) I like swimming the best.

11) I'm good at playing piano.

12) I'm a football fan.

13) I do enjoy playing cards.

14) I'm crazy about shopping.

15) I go to the cinema on weekends.

16) I like cleaning my apartment.

17) I enjoy cooking dinner for my family.

18) I go on the Internet.

19) I go for a walk.

20) **I'm addicted to** computer games.

Part 2 Taking up a new hobby

2.1 Prepare for group work

Walk around the classroom and find someone who... (You are going to interview at least 10 classmates.)

1) _____ is **crazy about** basketball.

Unit 7　Life Is a Hobby　　79

2) often **loses track of time** due to video games. _____

3) is **determined to** lose weight by playing badminton. _____

4) is **fed up with** Korean TV series. _____

5) enjoys cooking. _____

6) is **up for** traveling abroad. _____

7) **makes an effort** to learn a new sport. _____

8) **is into** rock music. _____

9) **goes jogging** regularly. _____

10) has ridden a motorcycle. _____

11) has been **scuba diving**. _____

12) has played tennis. _____

13) has **run a marathon**. _____

14) has **something in common** with you. _____

2.2　Watch

Watch a video and match the left column and the right column.

1. Thomas Edison	A. biking
2. Warren Buffet	B. collecting daggers
3. Barack Obama	C. Dungeons & Dragons
4. Beckham	D. fencing
5. Tim Duncan	E. golf
6. Steve Jobs	F. guitar
7. Brad Pitt	G. photography
8. Angelina Jolie	H. saxophone
9. Wright brothers	I. ukulele
10. Bill Clinton	J. silent movies

2.3　Work in pairs

Decide which activities are the cheapest, most expensive, most popular, etc.

chess	cosplay	cross-stitching	yoyo	cooking
go boating	**keeping pets**	**collecting coins**	sewing	ballet
skiing	knitting	**playing football**	hang-gliding	parachuting
scuba diving	**playing darts**	flying drones	trekking	hiking
doing DIY projects	**playing paintball**	collecting butterflies		

Which is/are...

the cheapest? _____

the most expensive? _____

the most popular? _____

the most exciting? _____

the dullest? _____

the most dangerous? _____

the most difficult? _____

the most tiring? _____

the most relaxing? _____

the most rewarding? _____

a complete waste of time? _____

Which one would you like to try?

_____

2.4 Work in pairs

What is your opinion?

Use the following starters to state your opinion.

- I think...
- I feel...
- I believe...
- I think it is fair to say...
- In my opinion...
- I think that depends on...

Unit 7 Life Is a Hobby 81

1) Watching TV makes people lazy and stupid.

2) Bungee jumping should be banned because it's a dangerous and crazy activity.

3) Playing video games encourages violent behavior among teenagers.

4) Students who play computer games perform poorly at school.

5) Young people should not play chess. It is **meant for** old people.

6) Playing football is more interesting than playing tennis.

2.5 Write

Listen and fill in the gaps.

Eric: Who were you talking to on the phone?

Melissa: My mother. I was **commiserating**(同情) with her about Dad's **retirement**.

Eric: Your father retired two months ago. That was a good thing, right?

Melissa: Well, it's good that he doesn't have to work anymore, but he's 1. _____. He 2. _____ the house and **gets in her way**. She retired last year, so she's had a year to establish her new routine. He's still 3. _____ lost.

Eric: Why doesn't he 4. _____? That would give him something interesting **to occupy his time**.

Melissa: Believe me, my mother has tried to 5. _____ gardening, woodworking, and even **scrapbooking**, but nothing has worked.

Eric: Those sound too **sedentary**(不爱活动的) for somebody as active as your father. How about encouraging him to **take up** bird watching or golf?

Melissa: He wouldn't be interested in those hobbies. I think he needs something more challenging, maybe **playing chess** or doing **genealogy**(family history). Maybe he could even learn to **play a** 6. _____.

Eric: Maybe your Dad just needs time to 7. _____ again. **Given time**, he'll **figure out** what he wants to do with his **newfound** free time.

Melissa: Maybe. But what does my mother do **in the meantime**?

Eric: She can **take up a new hobby**, too-out of the house!

Part 3　Talking about hobbies

3.1　Speak

Watch a video and summarize the main idea by using the following words.

competitive　　strengthen　　reflect　　make sure

_____

_____

3.2　Speak

What skills / qualities can you learn from certain hobbies?

1. swimming

2. speaking another language

3. writing stories and poems

4. dancing

5. playing the piano

6. cross-Stitch or knitting

7. building a model

8. playing basketball

9. flying drones

10. photography

11. yoga

12. scuba diving

3.3 Speak

Watch a video and answer the question "What does your hobby say about you?"

_____
_____
_____

Homework

My hobbies: past, present and future

In the past, I **used to** _____
_____

Nowadays, _____
_____

In the future, I'd like to try _____
_____

Hobbies are really important because _____

Part 4   Dialogues about hobbies

(1) Rachel: Would you like to go to a basketball game with me? You know, its funny, basketball, because I **happen to** have tickets, too. Umm, who likes the Knicks?

Joshua: What do you think?

Rachel: Oh! Well, as a single woman, who is available, I think you look great!

Joshua: Huh. Yeah?

Rachel: Yep. Oh, yeah, **you look great**. Oh yeah. Yeah, this looks great. Umm, so you like it?

Joshua: I do. I do. I love it. In fact, I think I'm gonna wear it home.

Rachel: Great.

Joshua: All right, thank you so much for all your help.

Rachel: Sure.

Joshua: Well, I guess this is... uh, I guess **this is it.**

Rachel: Yeah-eah-ha!

Joshua: Thanks. Maybe I'll see in the spring, with the... uh, you know, for the... uh, bathing suits.

Rachel: Oh well, you don't want to do that now?!

Joshua: Ah, that's okay, thanks.

Rachel: Okay.

Joshua: Anyway, hopefully, I'll **see you around sometime.**

Rachel: Basketball!

Joshua: Sorry.

Rachel: I... uh, I have two tickets to the Knicks game tonight if you're interested, just as a thank you for this week.

Joshua: Wow! That would be great.

Rachel: Really?

Joshua: Yeah, that would be fantastic! My nephew is **crazy about** the Knicks! This is fantastic, thank you so much, Rachel.

(2) Kevin: Hey, man! **What's up**?

Daniel: What's up?

Kevin: I'm tired. Just came back from football practice.

Daniel: Okay, so is football your favorite sport?

Kevin: Not really, no. I love football but my favorite sport is basketball. I can play it **all day long.**

Daniel: You should **try out** the basketball team then.

Kevin: Nah! I love basketball, but I don't play that well.

(3) Jessica: Hi, Kayla. What are you doing?

Kayla: Hey. Nothing much. I'm bored. I don't know what to do.

Jessica: How can a girl ever be bored? That's why mankind invented malls.

Don't you like to go to the mall?

Kayla: Is that so? I am **not much of** a shopping person.

Jessica: **Who said** anything about shopping? I like to **hang out** in the malls in my free time.

Kayla: That sounds better. I like to read books when I'm free. But I've got no new books to read.

Jessica: **No wonder** you get A's in all subjects.

(4) Ashton: What do you do for fun, Ryan?

Ryan: I like going out to watch new movies with my friends. What about you?

Ashton: I really like to go ice-skating. I go once or twice every month.

Ryan: We should **hang out together** sometime. Do both things.

Ashton: Yeah! Sure.

(5) Bethany: What do you do on the weekends?

Cory: We usually **hang out** at my place and **play video games**. What about you?

Bethany: My friends and I **go out**. This week we've planned a Karaoke night.

Cory: Oh, I've never tried that.

Bethany: You should join us. You may find out you like it.

Cory: I think you're right!

(6) Stephen: So, what do you do when you are bored?

Katy: I like watching movies. What about you?

Stephen: I like to bake.

Katy: Wow, that's very nice!

Stephen: Yep, it's a useful hobby.

Katy: I'm sure it is. And your family must love it!

Stephen: (laughing) Sure they do. They love the treats I bake for them.

(7) Hey, Peggy McKee with Career Confidential handling those **tough** (job interview) **questions**. Now the one I have here today, I don't think, is that tough. It

says, what are your hobbies? Well, this is easy. **Name off** a few of your hobbies, right? **Make sure** though that your hobbies reflect positively in your job. My hobbies are, I'm extremely... uh... I love to **be outdoors**, like playing with my kids. I'm competitive, like competing in horse events, like dogs, like cats... I love to read, consuming all kinds of material reading.

So see, this works for my job. You need to talk about hobbies that work for your job. If you have an extremely competitive job, you probably don't want to talk about being a crocheting person because that doesn't **strike people as** competitive. So they wanna see hobbies that reflect that competitiveness if that's what's important. If you're older, you wanna talk about hobbies that show that you have **high energy**, like marathons or walking or whatever it is that you do that shows that you have a lot of energy. Also technology. Are you a part of a technology club? Were you very interested in certain types of technology? That's gonna help with that question about ages that you're getting. So hobbies can help you strengthen the story about you as a (job) candidate.

I've also written a blog about this at careerconfidential. com/blog or you can **click on** the link below this video to get there immediately. **Best of luck!**

Part 5　My own dictionary

Look up in the dictionary

Use the first line for definitions, the second line for sentence examples.

1. all day long _____
   _____

2. addicted to _____
   _____

3. crazy about _____
   _____

4. determined to _____
   _____

Unit 7 Life Is a Hobby

5. fed up with

6. fond of

7. is into

8. outdoors

9. up for

10. wild about

11. Best of luck!

12. collect coins/ butterflies, etc.

13. drive sb up the wall

14. due to

15. football fan

16. Given time,...

17. hang out

18. happen to

19. have something in common

20. high energy

21. in the meantime

22. kind of

23. lose track of time

24. make an effort

25. meant for

26. No wonder...

27. scuba diving

28. See you around sometime.

29. This is it.

30. click on

31. figure out

32. find one's footing

33. interest sb. in

34. keep pets

35. strike people as

36. take a great interest in

37. take up a hobby

Unit 8 Culture Awareness

Part 1 What is culture?

1.1 *Watch*

Watch two videos and point out the cultural blunders made by Jack(film: *Mr. Baseball*)and Rich, Waverly's boyfriend(film: *The Joy Luck Club*).

The Joy Luck Club (1993)

The next week I brought Rich to Mom's birthday dinner, **sort of** *a surprise present. I figured she was going to have to accept Rich*, **like it or not**.

—Oh, Rich, this is my father.

—How ya doin'?

—Happy birthday, Mom.

—How are you?

—I'm good, thank you.

—And, Ma, this is Rich.

—Great to meet you.

—Boy, something smells wonderful.

—I guess we came to the right place, huh? Here you are.

—You know, Waverly has been telling me that you are the best cook.

I think maybe we got her.

—So many spots on his face.

Of course, the night was still young. Thank god I already prepped him on the Emily Post of Chinese manners.

—Hi, Uncle. How are you?

*Actually, there were a few things I **forgot to mention**.*

—Uh, let me **make a toast.**

*He **shouldn't have** had that second glass when everyone else had had only half an inch... just for taste.*

—Here's to everyone in the family.

—Shrimp! My favorite.

*He **should have** taken only a small spoonful of the best dish until everyone had had a helping.*

—He has **good appetite.**

*He **shouldn't have** bragged he was a **fast learner**. But the worst was when Rich criticized my mother's cooking and he didn't even know what he had done. As is the Chinese cook's custom, my mother always insults her own cooking but only with the dishes she serves with special pride.*

—This dish is not salty enough. No flavor. It's too bad to eat. But please...

***That was our cue** to eat some and proclaim it the best she'd ever made.*

—You know, Lindo... all this needs a little soy sauce.

—So, how'd your mom react when you told her about the wedding?

—It never **came up.**

—**How come**?

—She'd rather get rectal cancer.

1.2　Read

Read the passages.

Passage 1

Cameroon is a country in Central Africa with a population of approximately 20 million people. Cameroon shares its borders with Nigeria, Chad, Central African Republic, Congo. A small area of the country borders the Atlantic Ocean. The official languages of Cameroon are French and English, but over 200 different ethnic/linguistic groups populate the country. The literacy rate is close to 70% although it is higher among boys than girls as many girls must leave school early due to local customs. Health conditions are poor and there are few doctors. Nearly 70% of the population are farmers. Coco and coffee are the leading agricultural exports.

Can you imagine what kind of country Cameroon is? What is their culture? Is it similar to China?

Passage 2

We had a three-day weekend recently to Mt. Cameroon. We **set a time** with the bus driver the day before-8:00am. At 9:15, I went to the driver's house to get him. Finally, we were all on the bus, but we still faced more delays. First, the driver needed to buy petrol. Why didn't he do that yesterday? Then at the petrol station he started talking to some friends. Come on! If he stopped to chat with whoever he met, we'd never get there. One of my friends reminded me that socializing is **an essential part of** Cameroon's culture. Friends and relationships are so important here. **It stands to reason that** if you **run into** someone you know, you'll spend time talking to him. I value my friends too, but sometimes when faced with work or school, I ignore them. And you know what? We got there in plenty of time, and Mt. Cameroon was outstanding.

1. What difficulty did the traveler have?

2. What caused this difficulty?

3. What values are common in the traveler's home country but are different in Cameroon?

Part 2 Importance of cultural awareness

2.1 Watch

Watch videos and fill in the blanks.

Wedding Presents

In England, presents are given to the bride and groom to 1. _____ in their new life. Whereas in Malta, guests can expect a present as memento of the day.

Commuting, Dining, Guests

In some Asian cities, it's 2. _____ for a commuter to fall asleep on the shoulder of a stranger. In New York, it's quite 3. _____ of course, you could always adapt.

The English believe it's a slur on your host's food if you don't 4. _____, whereas the Chinese feel that you 5. _____ my generosity if you do.

In America, if you had a hole-in-one you're expected to buy everyone a drink. However, in Japan, it's traditional to buy your 6. _____ expensive gifts.

Flowers

In Italy, different flowers have different meanings: chrysanthemums, for example, are 7. _____ funerals and sadness.

It's not that common for...to...

It's normal to...

They'd need to know that whenever we...

If they don't want to stand out too much, they'd have to...

2.2 Write

Study the sentences. Which expressions pertain to similarities? Differences?

Write your answers below.

1. The two cultures are **fundamentally similar.**
2. North Korea **bears little resemblance to** South Korea.
3. There is **a wide variation of** cuisine in China.
4. The two cultures are **entirely different.**
5. The two cultures are **strikingly different.**
6. The two cultures are **exact opposite.**
7. The two cultures are **polar opposite.**
8. The Japanese have a high context culture which is **in marked contrast to** Americans.
9. There is **a world of difference** when it comes to food in America and food in China.
10. There is **a clear distinction between** the country and city landscapes.
11. There is **a wide gap between** Arab and western cultures.

Mediterranean and Latin cultures **differ widely.**

Words that mean "similar"	Words that mean "different"

2.3 Work in pairs

Watch a video about British and Chinese cultures. Take notes by filling in the chart. Then summarize in your own words using the phrases you have just learned.

	British culture	Chinese culture
Food		
Drink		
Class		
Boy-girl relationships		

Unit 8　Culture Awareness

续表

	British culture	Chinese culture
Dress		
Pets		
Shops		
Gay bars		

Part 3　Right attitude

3.1　Write

Write Yes or No on the blanks.

1. We need to recognize and welcome **cultural diversity**. _____

2. Cultural awareness **begins with** self-awareness. _____

3. **Make assumptions** about other people. _____

4. **Make judgments** about people even if we don't understand their culture. _____

5. We certainly don't need empathy to understand the other person. _____

6. Just forget that people **new to** living in your culture **face challenges** we can only imagine. _____

7. You don't have to **agree with** the views of others, but always respect them. _____

8. When we learn to **embrace the differences** between us, we can work well together. _____

9. **Keeping language simple** helps prevent the exclusion of others. _____

10. It's a mistake to try to **impose** one culture onto another. _____

3.2　Work in pairs

Work with a partner. You have two intercultural dilemmas and your partner has two different ones. Take turns to describe the dilemmas to each other and discuss what you'd do in each situation. Do you agree on what you should do? Is it what you'd both really do?

Speaker A

Dilemma 1: You meet a Spanish business contact you haven't seen **for ages** who wants to stop and chat, but you're **running late** for an appointment. Do you stay or do you **make your excuses** and go?

Dilemma 2: A British salesman is giving you a demonstration of a new office product. He seems to like telling a lot of jokes. Do you join in the joke-telling or wait until he **gets to the point**?

Speaker B

Dilemma 3: Your new American boss organizes a weekend barbeque. You find yourself amongst a lot of people you've never met. Do you join in the fun or leave as early as you can?

Dilemma 4: You are having a pre-negotiation coffee at a potential client's headquarters in Berlin. Do you **mingle with** the opposing team or stick with your own people?

Homework

In groups, prepare a PPT about the culture of your own choice. Be reminded of the different aspects of culture as explained by your teacher. Present your work in class.

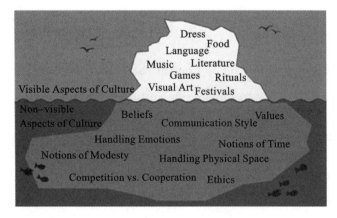

Part 4 My own dictionary

Look up in the dictionary

Use the first line for definitions, the second line for sentence examples.

1. a clear distinction between _____

   _____

2. a different story _____

   _____

3. a wide gap between _____

   _____

4. a wide variation of _____

   _____

5. a world of difference _____

   _____

6. agree with _____

   _____

7. an essential part _____

   _____

8. associate with _____

   _____

9. bear little resemblance to _____

   _____

10. begin with _____

    _____

11. clear one's plate _____

    _____

12. be considered acceptable _____

    _____

13. cultural diversity

14. differ widely

15. embrace the differences

16. entirely different

17. exact opposite

18. face challenges

19. fast learner

20. for ages

21. forget to mention

22. fundamentally similar

23. get to the point

24. good appetite

25. How come...?

26. in marked contrast to

27. It stands to reason that...

Unit 8 Culture Awareness

28. It's normal to...

29. It's not that common for... to...

30. like it or not

31. make a toast

32. make an excuse

33. make an assumption

34. make judgment

35. mingle with

36. new to

37. polar opposite

38. run into

39. running late

40. set a time

41. set somebody up

42. should/ shouldn't have

43. sort of

44. strikingly different

45. That was our cue...

46. to come up

Unit 9　Creative Selling

Part 1　How to sell a product

Work in pairs

(1) The following factors are necessary for success in selling a company's product/service. Determine their degree of importance by putting a tick mark (√) on the corresponding blank.

	Important	Extremely important
1. Company reputation	_____	_____
2. Promptness of delivery	_____	_____
3. Quality of product/service	_____	_____
4. Completeness of product line	_____	_____
5. Promptness of support, service	_____	_____
6. Manuals and other supporting literature	_____	_____
7. Price	_____	_____
8. Skills of sales reps	_____	_____
9. Technical support	_____	_____
10. Personal relationships	_____	_____
11. Brochures and other promotional literature	_____	_____

(2) Work in groups and discuss some of the techniques which advertisers use to persuade the public to buy their products. Give examples from advertisements you know. Compare your list of techniques with the following ones:

1. Testimonials from famous people to build confidence in a product;
2. Drawing on higher/expert authority to prove claims;

3. The down-to-earth approach based on the idea of an ordinary, honest person who recognizes quality and isn't easily duped;

4. Repetition of claims which are not necessarily based on reality;

5. Use of humor;

6. Emphasizing value for money;

7. Exaggeration.

Part 2 Make it possible

2.1 Write

Watch a video '*Dream it possible*' and see how Huawei tries to impress its potential customer. Fill in the blanks with words you hear.

> I will run, I will climb, I will (1) _____
> I'm undefeated
> Jumping out of my skin, pull the chord
> Yeah I (2) _____ it
> The past is everything we were,
> [they] don't make us who we are.
> So I'll (3) _____ until I make it real,
> and all I see is stars.
>
> It's not until you (4) _____ that you fly
> When your dreams come alive you're (5) _____
> Take a shot, chase the sun, find the beautiful
> We will (6) _____ in the dark turning dust to gold
> And we'll dream it possible.
>
> I will (7) _____, I will reach, I will fly
> Until I'm breaking, until I'm breaking
> Out of my (8) _____, like a bird in the night

Unit 9　Creative Selling   103

> I know I'm changing, I know I'm changing
>
> In-into something big, better than before
>
> And if it takes, takes a thousand lives
>
> Then it's worth (9) _____
>
> ...
>
> From the bottom to the top
>
> We're sparking wild fires
>
> Never (10) _____ and never stop
>
> The rest of our lives.

2.2　Answer the following questions.

(1) Why is the girl crying on the bus?

A. She is excited to leave her home that's like a cage.

B. She is happy to go out to a big city.

C. She is sad to leave her family.

D. She doesn't have a smart phone.

(2) Which of the following statements about the girl is NOT true?

A. She found it hard to play the piano and thought of quitting.

B. She was sad to leave her dear grandpa.

C. She grew up into a success.

D. She worked for Huawei.

(3) Which of the following statements does NOT describe Huawei?

A. Huawei aims to connect people.

B. Huawei tries to run, climb and soar.

C. Huawei has been changing into something big and better than before

D. Huawei isolates people as everyone is busy with their phones

(4) The video is an advertisement by Huawei. What do you think of this advertisement?

A. It goes into my heart.

B. It is a waste of money.

C. It is not selling.

D. It conveys nothing.

E. Other (_____)

(5) What feelings/emotions are aroused in you by this commercial? Share your ideas with your friend. The following words are for your reference.

love   hatred   jealousy   envy   connection

isolation   optimism   pessimism   determination   perseverance

(6) The commercial you have just watched use the following advertising techniques. Find evidence or facts for each technique

1) Using simple words.

_____

2) Same structure is repeated.

_____

3) Same sounds/words are repeated.

_____

Part 3   How to think outside of the box

3.1   Speak

Watch a video and describe what happened and your reaction.

3.2   Read

Ways to be more creative.
- Alphabetize adventure.
- Add up a series of one-digit number... fast.
- Turn the problem upside down.
- Be open to all possibilities.
- Get outside your comfort zone.

Unit 9 Creative Selling

You are late for school and your teacher is very angry. Could you come up with some creative excuses to make your teacher pardon you?

_____

_____

Part 4 Red Dot Award

4.1 Prepare for group work

In order to keep up with the competition, your company must come up with a new product that is going to define the new age. In groups, brainstorm ideas following the guidelines below.

- To brainstorm a list of ten common objects.
- To brainstorm ten materials.
- To consider the two lists and speculate on the most unlikely combinations of materials and objects, for example, *a wooden balloon*. You are going to prepare an advertisement for this product.

Materials	Products / Services	Functions / Features
plastic	carpet	ease the pain
metal	watch	work more effectively
cotton	violin	more beautiful
glass	phone	various colors to choose
water	cup	large display
paper	tableware	lightweight

Your product presentation should include the following parts. Try to use the phrases you've learnt to describe your designing process.

- Our product is made of _____.
- It can be used / serve as _____.

- Special features include _____.
- It is unique because _____.

4.2 Watch

Watch a video and understand the difference between features and benefits.

Features	Benefits
It is very _____.	It's child _____.
It's twelve inches _____.	This long pipe _____ your hand _____ from the flame so you never _____.
It's _____ red.	It's easy to find in the _____.
It has a _____.	You don't have to _____ children playing with it.
It _____ ten dollars.	You can _____ buy one for all your family and friends.

4.3 Write

Use the following sentence structures to sell your brilliant products.

- You can _____.
- You can afford to _____.
- You don't have to _____.
- It's easy to _____.

Part 5 Ways for your reference to be more creative

Read

- **Alphabetize adventure**

First, think of any word or see a word on a magazine cover or billboard (preferably six or so letters). Second, stop and look at the word and just picture it in your mind. Then arrange all the letters in your head so they are in alphabetical order. So, for example, take a word like NUMBER. You would spell it as follows: B E M N R U. Try this for five minutes a day, three days a week. You'll notice after a while, your mind will be used to looking at things **in a different way** and you've come up with ideas that **you've never thought of before**.

- **Add up a series of one-digit numbers... fast**

Adding up small numbers in your head quickly ($4+7+9+2+8+6+1...$) compels you to continually change the information that you are having to work with and remember. It is very helpful in training the mind to remember essential information while deleting other details when they are **no longer** needed. So the next time when you're standing in line and you're tempted to whip out your cell phone, why don't you instead whip out a bill and add up the serial number **as fast as possible**?

- **Turn the problem upside down**

For example, if you want to be a better manager, then you would ask, "What would someone do each day if he was a terrible manager?" This line of questioning will often reveal some **surprising insights**. For example, say you want to increase your focus and productivity. You could ask, "What if I wanted to decrease my focus? What are ways I could distract myself?" The answer to that question may help you discover distractions you can eliminate, which should also increase your **level of productivity**.

- **Be open to all possibilities**

Avoid saying things such as **"That won't work"**, "We haven't done it that way before", "We can't solve this problem", "We don't have enough time." It will **shut down** creativity rather than encourage it.

- **Get outside your comfort zone**

The comfort zone is a psychological state in which a person feels familiar, **at ease**, in control, and experiences low anxiety. View your comfort zone not as a shelter but a prison. Embrace constructive discomfort. Don't take the safe, known path. Lean into the discomfort. Don't sprint out of your comfort zone; take small but frequent steps. Push the walls out; don't try to knock them down. Maybe you can do something outside your comfort zone. Today, try to wear a ridiculous costume, tell jokes to strangers, sing the names of each stop on the subway.

Part 6　My own dictionary

Look up in the dictionary

Use the first line for definitions, the second line for sentence examples.

1. company reputation _____

2. promptness of delivery _____

3. personal relationships _____

4. build confidence _____

5. down-to-earth approach _____

6. value for money _____

7. use of humor _____

8. special features _____

9. in a different way _____

10. never thought of before _____

11. no longer _____

12. as fast as possible _____

13. surprising insights

14. level of productivity

15. That won't work.

16. shut down

17. comfort zone

18. at ease

19. out of date

20. brand new

21. I wonder…

22. dress up

23. for no good reason

24. set fire

25. keep something as a pet

26. run across

27. on the edge of

Unit 10 Job Interview

Part 1 Different jobs

1.1 Work in pairs

In pairs, guess which job is referred to in the following sentences.

1. I serve food in a restaurant.

2. I'm responsible for welcoming and helping people who visit our company.

3. One of my duties is helping guests who arrive at our hotel.

4. I have excellent communication skills. I'm also good at **following up** on prospective customers and know exactly when to push.

5. I have very good observation skills and pay extreme attention to detail. I also have a love for adventure and am very brave.

6. I'm an excellent motivator. I have a way of getting the most out of my subordinates and inspiring them to work hard and develop the company.

7. I have **excellent interpersonal skills** and am very persuasive. I also possess good public speaking skills and I'm very comfortable addressing a room full of people.

1.2 Read

Match the descriptions to their opposites.

1. It's very tedious.	A. It's a piece of cake.
2. It can be very stressful.	B. It's badly-paid.
3. It's well-paid.	C. It's exciting and interesting.
4. You work long hours.	D. It's usually very relaxing.
5. It's very challenging.	E. It's very safe.
6. It can be very hectic.	F. There's usually nothing to do.

7. You meet lots of people.   G. You can go home early.

8. It can be dangerous.   H. You don't need a degree.

9. You need very good qualifications.   I. You feel very isolated.

There are so many jobs that you can do, such as actors, accountants, chefs, vets. In pairs, have a conversation about any jobs. Ask your partner if he/she would like to do the jobs. Answer with "yes, definitely", "maybe", "not really" or "definitely not". Explain your answers using the phrases from 1.2. For example:

A: *Would you like to be an actor?*

B: *Yes, definitely. It seems like an exciting and well-paid job.*

1.3 Write

Number the following in order of how important you think they are, with number 1 as the most important. You can add others if they are important to you.

- ◆A high salary
- ◆A pleasant working environment
- ◆Regular challenges
- ◆Responsibility
- ◆Recognition for my achievements
- ◆The chance to travel
- ◆Job satisfaction
- ◆Promotion opportunities
- ◆Independence
- ◆Power and authority

1.4 Write

Rank these skills in order of how important you think they are for your job or career.

- ◆Organization
- ◆Problem-solving
- ◆Working under pressure
- ◆Anger management
- ◆Assertiveness
- ◆Communication
- ◆Creativity
- ◆Critical thinking
- ◆Decision making
- ◆Leadership
- ◆Negotiating
- ◆Networking
- ◆Self-awareness
- ◆Teamwork
- ◆Time management

Part 2 Job interview

2.1 Read

What companies require from the employees.

- ◆committed
- ◆competent
- ◆creative
- ◆flexible
- ◆honest
- ◆organized
- ◆experienced
- ◆self-motivated
- ◆communicative
- ◆enthusiastic
- ◆dynamic
- ◆hardworking
- ◆listening to people
- ◆open-minded
- ◆optimistic

2.2 Watch

Watch a video about successful interviews and write down the tips.

1.

2.

3.

4.

5.

6.

7.

8.

2.3 Read

What is "STAR"?

STAR stands for:

• **Situation**—Provide some brief details about the situation you were in when you used a competency so that the reader can understand the context of the example.

• **Task**—Outline what your objective or purpose was during that situation, again to put your answer into context.

• **Action**—Describe what you did in that situation and how you approached it.

• **Result**—State the outcome, for example: Were the objectives met? What did you learn/gain from being in that situation?

2.4 Work in pairs

Match the following answers with the questions.

1. **I would describe myself as** someone who is ambitious, hardworking and motivated by challenges.

2. As you can see from my CV, I've been working as a project partner for the company branch in Rome for several years.

3. **My job has mainly involved** organizing special events.

4. **Against the odds,** I managed to successfully work with our partners and reschedule the project events.

5. I guess at times I am a little reluctant to delegate certain tasks.

6. **I would say** successfully completing my university degree has been my most rewarding accomplishment.

7. **My long-term goals involve** growing with a company where I can continue to learn, and take on additional responsibilities.

8. **Once I gain necessary experience,** I see myself moving on to a management position.

A. describing your current job

B. describing your personal qualities

C. describing a personal weakness

D. describing how you overcome a difficult situation

E. describing your ambitions

F. describing your achievements

2.5 Read

Expect the unexpected.

Sometimes the interviewers ask questions that are so unusual. You'd never predict they'd come up in an interview. This is often done to test how quickly you can think on your feet and to see how well you respond when put under a bit of pressure. Examples include:

• If I were an alien, just landed on earth, what do you think are the three key issues I would need to know?

• In a news story about your life, what would the headline be?

• If you won £20 million on the Lotto, what would you spend the money on?

• If you were a piece of fruit, what sort of fruit would you be?

• If you could change one thing about yourself, what would it be?

The trick when answering these questions is firstly, don't panic, and secondly, to think about how you can use the opportunity to demonstrate a positive personal characteristic or skill that you know the recruiter is looking for. Here is an attempt at answering an unexpected question.

What sort of fruit would you choose to be?

I would choose to be an orange as they have a bright welcoming color that makes them stand out. My recent work experience as a supermarket assistant showed that it was important to be welcoming, helpful and friendly towards customers at all times. Oranges are also the shape of a ball which I associate with my love of football and being a good team player. I think an orange has hidden depths and values that you only discover once it is peeled.

2.6 Prepare for group work

Interview practice—have a go! Try this role-play or mock interview exercise with one or two friends.

In your group, you can each take turns to assume the role of a candidate with others acting as the interviewers and observers. Conduct a 10-minute interview. The observers should keep time, along with making notes on your performance. Spend 5—10 minutes discussing the feedback: you first (saying how you thought it went), then your friends (remember the positive feedback).

Commonly asked questions:

1. Why do you want to do this job?

2. What do you know about our organization?

3. Why would you find us interesting to work for?

4. Which aspects of the job interest you most?

5. What do you think will be the main challenges of this job? Why does that appeal to you?

6. What steps have you taken to find out more about the job role?

7. Which aspects of your previous work experience have you enjoyed and why?

8. Tell us about a current news story that has caught your attention and why it interests you. How might it relate to our organization?

9. Give an example of when you worked in a team to complete a task. What was your role and what did you contribute?

10. Tell us about a situation where you've had to overcome a difficult problem.

11. Describe an occasion when you have had to manage your time to achieve a deadline. What happened and how did you meet the deadline?

12. Tell us about a time when you have had to deal with someone who was angry or upset. How did you deal with it?

Part 3 Scripts for your reference

(1)

I think once you get to the interview stage, you've already shown us that you've got the skills and background in order to either be on the course or do the job. An interview really is an opportunity for you to show that you're genuine, that you're passionate, you're enthusiastic—and those are things you really can't **get across** on paper. So when you're preparing for your interview, have a think about the things that you can exhibit in person, that you can't articulate that way. Well, I think **first and foremost**, it's absolutely crucial that you be yourself. There can be a great temptation to try and tell us what you think we want to hear, and that doesn't work. Be yourself because if you put on a bit of an act, that often comes through in an interview. If you're being yourself, it's much easier to **build rapport** with whoever you're interviewing as well. Just focus on the basics. So what I mean by that is first impressions, because they do really last. So make sure that you are dressed to impress. Always err on the side of caution for an interview. **Dress smart.** Give yourself a good impression. Shirt and tie, smart business dress, those kind of things. If you are not entirely sure what you should wear, don't be afraid to ask the person who's coordinating the recruitment process.

You need to really **make good eye contact** with the people who are interviewing you. And you really need to run with any questions. So that means that if they ask you a question, you don't give kind of a one-or a two-word answer. You give the full answer and then push that answer a little bit further. So take it back to the people that are interviewing you. So in that way, you're showing that you're engaged with the topic. Be passionate. It is the thing that certainly in a graduate recruitment market can make graduates stand out and something organizations are absolutely looking for. We don't want people who can just recite things that they've read. We want people that have a passion or a connection to what they want. Understand what the company is. Demonstrate you have a personality that will **fit well into** our team, because that's the most important thing. Because we're putting teams of people together and we're working in a really stressful environment. Personality is just so key. Well, one of the most important things is making sure you do the preparation. Preparation. Know the market, know the industry, know the company, and know the job that you're **applying for.** It's really important that you have some idea of the institutions to which you've applied. If you applied to the University of Sheffield, that's fantastic. But if you are applying to any medical school, you should know something about that school and about its course. Prepare, prepare, prepare. You cannot do enough preparation. And in interviewing people, it's the thing that lets them down the most. If you go for a job interview, say you've managed to get through the application stage, you're through that gate, you've got another gate to get through—really high competition. Employers these days are very choosy. If somebody doesn't **meet the criteria**, they're not a fit, they will not appoint them. So you really need to understand the role and the organization, sit with the job description, the person specification, make yourself lots of notes about how you meet it.

Try to think of some really good questions. And research the company so that when you go for the interview, you can show evidence that you know a little bit about it. So you might say, "Oh, I noticed on your website" or "I read a press article", something that just **gives you that edge**. Be familiar with your application form or CV. Most people who go to an interview or are interviewing you will have read that and be familiar with it. So be prepared to elaborate on the stories, further develop them, and make sure that they're truthful. Don't lie.

You'd be surprised the amount of people who put things in their application that unravels quite quickly at interview—and you will be found out. So just **stick to the truth**, be honest, and be personable. There's nothing worse in an interview than somebody trying to wing an answer. If you're working on a big piece of machinery, like a rolling mill, and you try and fumble your way through solving an issue, then there's going to be big problems. But for the really obvious questions, like, why do you want to apply for the job, why have you applied, what's your understanding of this, you should know that really well. And you should have practiced speaking about it beforehand. So just get a friend or a brother or whoever to sit down, ask a few of the questions that you think come up, and practice saying it to them so that you just feel so much more confident when you actually go in on the day. Try not to let nerves get the better of you. I think everybody appreciates that interviews can be really **nerve wracking**. But there are certain things that you can do to try and work on those nerves beforehand. And that's really down to preparation and practice. Practice as well.

Get your friends or family members to ask you interview questions and do a bit of practice beforehand so you're ready on the day and you can show that you're enthusiastic and you really want to work there and that comes across. If you are challenged by a particular question, you don't understand something, you need it repeating, ask for that to be the case. And make sure you're providing sufficient depth to your answers. One tip I've got for people who are doing interviews is to make sure your answers aren't too long. Bear in mind, the people interviewing you have been sat there all day or they're going to after they've finished with you. So entertain them a bit.

Tell them something they didn't know. Use the STAR technique when you're forming your interview questions and answers. When I ask you a question, think about the situation, the task, the action, and the result. If you form your answers like that, the interview will get everything that they need from what you're saying and they won't need to ask you as many follow-up questions. Really think about against each essential criteria on the person specification. How you could evidence it, but really actually write down what a STAR scenario would be. So what was the situation? What was the task that you specifically were asked to do? What did you do? But always be able to think of results. Do your best.

All you can do is your best, so aim for that. Aim for your best. And then you don't have to worry, you don't have to get too nervous. Just do your best and then you can leave the room thinking, yup, I did what I could. And if I get it, great. If I don't, there will be another opportunity.

(2)

STAR is an extremely useful tool to help you answer those **tricky questions** that **come up** on application forms and at interview. It stands for Situation, Task, Action and Result. A question may start as "Give an example of when..." or "Tell me about a situation where..." Start by providing some details about the situation, so that the reader or interviewer can understand the context of your example. Next, identify the task; what needed to be done. Then describe the action that you took; what did you do and how did you do it? And finally, describe the result. You could even go on to describe what you learned or gained from it.

So for example, the interviewer or application form might say "Give an example of when you've worked as part of a team to solve a problem." First, describe the situation. "I'm the captain of the Sheffield Holts, a local women's football team. And we recently played in the final of the Carly Cup against Leeds Lock. At half-time we were losing by two goals to one." Then identify the task. "This was the first time we'd ever reached the final and we needed to win to help us raise our profile and try to secure financial sponsorship for the following season. It was clear that I needed to rethink our team formation, motivate the players and raise morale."

Next, you'll need to walk through the actions you made. "Realizing that the other team was stronger than us in mid-field, I reorganized the team to play five in the mid-field, detailing our strongest defender to mark their strongest forward closely to stop her from getting into a forward position. Reminding the team that we had a better record for scoring goals over the season compared to our opposition improved their confidence and lifted their morale." Finally, describe the result. "By applying these changes and encouraging the team throughout the second half, we managed to break through their mid-field and scored two goals to win the cup. We also secured financial sponsorship for the next season ensuring that we can continue playing."

Part 4　My own dictionary

Look up in the dictionary

Use the first line for definitions, the second line for sentence examples.

1. good qualifications

2. need a degree

3. not really

4. definitely not

5. a high salary

6. recognition for my achievement

7. promotion opportunities

8. decision making

9. time management

10. My job has mainly involved...

11. against the odds

12. My long-term goals involve...

13. gain necessary experience

14. get across

15. first and foremost

16. build rapport

17. dress smart

18. make good eye contact

19. fit well into

20. apply for

21. meet the criteria

22. give you that edge

23. stick to the truth

24. nerve-wracking

25. come across

26. sufficient depth

27. aim for your best

28. tricky question

29. come up